Encyclopedia of
Antique
AMERICAN
Clocks

Robert W. & Harriett Swedberg

Published by

**krause
publications**

700 E. State Street • Iola, WI 54990-0001
Telephone: 715/445-2214

Please call or write for our free catalog of publications.
Our toll-free number to place an order or obtain a free catalog is 800-258-0929
or please use our regular business telephone 715-445-2214.

ISBN: 0-87349-273-0
Library of Congress Catalog Number: 2001086367

Printed in the United States of America

Dedication

We dedicate this book to our two-year-old grandson, Edy Rodolfo Thurston Swedberg, who has filled our lives with happiness and love; and to our friend, Dennis Roberts, an advanced clock collector, whom we deeply thank for providing us with direction and information in the development of this book and our preceeding clock text, *Price Guide to Antique Clocks*.

Table of Contents

Acknowledgments

The authors sincerely thank the following collectors and dealers who assisted in obtaining photographs and information for this book. We also thank those clock collectors who allowed us to include some of their photographed clocks but did not wish to be listed.

Annawan Antique Alley
Mary Wheeler
Annawan, Illinois

Antique America
Cheryle Fry
Davenport, Iowa

Antique Mall
Shafer & Sons Clock Co.
Rockford, Illinois

Antique & Specialty Center
Don and Sharon Hanebuth
Anchorage, Alaska

Antique Scene
Rachel and Jack Cattrell
Moline, Illinois

Marion and Vera Blevins

Gary Bowker

Richard and Norma Broline

Bill and Dora Brubaker

Butterworth Clock Repair
Mark Buttrerworth,
Muscatine, Iowa

Chuck Cline

James Stanley Feehan
Joy, Illinois

Bennie L. Hack
Decatur, Illinois

Pastor Troy C. Hedrick

Jack Heilsler

Scott Helmich

Carmon M. and Peggy M. Howe

The Illinois Antique Center
Dan and Kim Philips
Peoria, Illinois

J. & S. Antiques & Mall
Jim and Sandy Boender
Manlius, Illinois

Mort Jacobs Restorations
Chicago, Illinois

Shirley Kilgard

David and Emily Lewis
Specializing in Kroeber clocks
Western Illinois

The Louisville Antique Mall
Harold L., Chuck, and Don Sego
Louisville, Kentucky

Michael and Patricia Lowe

Bill and Sandy Mittelstadt
Oldest Son's Antiques and Appraisal Service
Nancy, Jerry and helper Jason
Pocahontas, Illinois

Old Timers-Antique Clocks
Dick Masters
Louisville Antique Mall
Louisville, Kentucky

Peerless Antiques & Auctions
Chris Wojtanowski
Rock Island, Illinois

Terry and Gretchen Poffinbarger

Pritts Antiques
Talvia and Theral
Decatur, Illinois

Dennis and Barbara Roberts

Ken Russell
Antique Clocks & Repair
Lacon, Illinois

Smokehouse Square Antiques
Ken and Lesley Denzin
Amana, Iowa

Barry and Lori Snodgrass

John Tanner
Chino, California

Mariam Thornton

Village Square Antiques
Theresa and Glen Nance
Pocahontas, Illinois

Chapter 1

An Overall View of Clock Types

Pictured in this chapter are examples of the different types of clocks that are shown and priced throughout this book. These examples are arranged alphabetically, and the clock type is in bold face, followed by other information on the particular example.

ALARM CLOCK *Left, Ansonia flower girl alarm clock, 7" high; $375. Right, Ansonia cupid alarm clock, 6-1/2" high; $400.*

ADVERTISING (WALL) CLOCK *Sessions walnut Jeweler's regulator wall clock, 1902, advertising Weiler's Music Store, Quincy, Illinois, time only, 38-1/2" high; $650.*

BANJO CLOCK *Sessions Clock Company mahogany finished banjo wall clock with Sessions on dial, eight-day, time and strike, 6" dial, 10-1/2" wide, 35" high; $275.*

BEEHIVE (Gothic Style) CLOCK E.N. Welch rosewood Gothic (beehive) shelf clock, all original, circa 1860 to 1870, 10-1/2" wide, 19" high; $350.

CABINET CLOCK Ansonia "Cabinet C" oak shelf clock, brass dial, ormolu decorations, turned oak columns and brass feet, eight-day, time and strike, 11-1/2" wide, 19" high; $1,000.

CALENDAR (Shelf) CLOCK Seth Thomas "Number 10" walnut perpetual calendar shelf clock with applied and turned decorations. Provisions for the date, day and month are on the lower round tablet, eight-day, time and strike, weight driven, 36" high; $4,000.

CARRIAGE CLOCK *Ansonia carriage clocks; left, has elliptical dial, 30-hour, time only, 2-1/2" wide, 6" high; $600. Right, "Oriole" enameled in colors, with brass framework, 30-hour, time and alarm, 6-1/2" high; $550.*

CUCKOO CLOCK *Unknown maker, multi-colored wooden pendulette cuckoo clock, 30-hour, time only, spring-driven; $65.*

CRYSTAL REGULATOR *Ansonia "Regal" crystal regulator, finished in rich gold, visible (or open) escapement, mercury pendulum, beveled glass, eight-day, half-hour gong strike, 10-1/2" wide, 18-1/2" high; $4,500.*

GALLERY CLOCK *Seth Thomas oak gallery wall clock, circa 1890, 30-day, time only, 24" diameter; $600.*

MANTEL CLOCK *Unmarked metal front mantel clock, patented Oct. 18, 1902, brass case with angel figure at top, 30-hour, time only, 8" wide, 10" high; $95.*

GRANDFATHER CLOCK *Unknown maker, mahogany grandfather clock with satinwood and mother-of-pearl inlay, double weight brass, silver and gold-leaf face, moving moon dial, 22" wide, 97" high; no price available.*

METAL FRONT CLOCK *Ansonia metal front mantel clock, gilded case, porcelain dial, eight-day, time and strike, 7-1/2" wide, 10-1/2" high; $250.*

MISSION STYLE CLOCK *Unknown maker, oak mission wall clock, exposed pendulum, 13" wide, 26" high; $295.*

MOTHER-OF-PEARL CASE CLOCK *Seth Thomas Plymouth Hollow cottage clock with mother-of-pearl decorated case, eight-day, time and strike, 11" wide, 17" high; $450.*

OAK SHELF CLOCK *W. L. Gilbert "Perfect" oak shelf clock, applied decorations and pressed designs, eight-day, time, strike, and alarm, 15" wide, 23-1/2" high; $350.*

OCTAGON CLOCK *New Haven embossed oak simple calendar wall clock, circa 1910, eight-day, time only, 17" wide, 28" high; $450.*

OG CLOCK *Seth Thomas mahogany OG, eight-day, time and strike, weight driven, 15" wide, 25" high; $275.*

PORCELAIN CLOCK *Ansonia Royal Bonn porcelain shelf clock with open escapement, porcelain dial, eight-day, time and strike, 13-1/2" wide, 15" high; $1,250.*

PARLOR CLOCK *Ansonia "Triumph" walnut parlor shelf clock, mirror sides with cupid statues, circa 1890, applied metal decorations, eight-day, time and strike, 17" wide, 24" high; $650.*

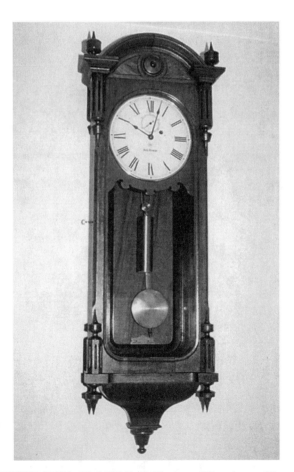

PAPIER MÂCHÉ CLOCK *William S. Johnson, New York, black-enameled papier-mâché case with mother-of-pearl inlay, circa 1895, eight-day, time and strike with winders below the dial, 11" wide, 17" high; $750.*

REGULATOR CLOCK *Seth Thomas "Regulator 6" oak wall clock, circa 1905, second hand, time only, brass weight and pendulum, 16" wide, 48" high; $2,200.*

STATUE CLOCK *New Haven statue clock with cupid, gilded metal, 30-hour, time only, 5" wide, 6-1/2" high; $350.*

STEEPLE CLOCK *E. N. Welch steeple shelf clock; left, rosewood case, circa 1880, 30-hour, time, strike, and alarm, 8" wide, 15" high; $250. Right, banded mahogany, circa 1880, 30-hour, time, strike and alarm, 10" wide, 19" high; $200.*

TRIPLE-DECKER CLOCK *C. & L. C. Ives Walnut triple-decker shelf clock, circa 1830, time and strike, weight driven, 38" high; $700.*

Chapter 2

A Brief History of Clock Making

The historical information and dates that follow present a succinct review of horological history. We have tried to show facts as accurately as our research permits, keeping in mind that sources sometimes differ on dates, names and other facts relevant to clock history.

885 — Candles were used as clocks; an idea introduced by Alfred the Great of England.

1300s

1360 — The first mechanical clock was constructed in France.

1380 — Italy produced the first domestic clocks.

1386 — England's earliest known public clock was installed at the Salisbury Cathedral. It had no hands but told the time by striking on the hours.

1500s

1500 — The mainspring was invented by Peter Henlein of Nurnberg.

1525 — Fusee was invented by Jacob the Czech.

1530 — Screws for metal work became available.

Circa 1584 — Galileo (1564-1642), an astronomer, physicist and college professor, born in Pisa, Italy, is credited with discovering the properties of the pendulum. Galileo was a 20-year old college student (according to some sources, slightly younger) when on a visit to the city's cathedral, he watched a suspended lamp swinging to and fro. Timing it with the beat of his pulse, he discovered that a short swing moved slowly while a long one moved more rapidly. Because of this, the time taken for the completion of a swing back and forth was the same for both.

1600s

Early 1600s — Pendulums with anchor or dead-beat escapement replaced the less accurate foliot balance. Among the colonists who settled in 1607 and 1620 were skilled workers, including those with clock making knowledge. They made clocks one at a time, relying on England for their supplies.

1607 — The first successful settlement in North America was established at Jamestown, in what is now the state of Virginia.

1640 — The manufacture of Black Forest clocks began.

Circa 1650 — The first American tower clock was completed in Boston.

1657 — Dutch scientist, Christiaan Huygens, created the first pendulum based on Galileo's observations. The pendulum's back and forth swinging motion served as a clock's regulating mechanism. This inventor's name is spelled in various ways by different authors. Most spell his first name with one "a" while his last name has been seen as "Huijghens," "Huygens" or "Huyghens."

1660 — The balance or hairspring came into use.

1673-1771 — George Graham's two essential contributions to clock making were the dead-beat escapement and the mercurial compensation pendulum.

1680 — Second hands made their first appearance.

Late 1600s — A London-made grandfather clock cost about $57. Its ebony case had fancy carving and gilded metal-applied decorations. It could also have been made of walnut.

1700s

1700-1799 — Clocks appeared in homes as a mark of prosperity.

1715 — The deadbeat escapement for use on regulator clocks was invented.

1716 — A public clock built by Joseph Phillips tolled the news of Washington's inauguration in New York City.

1721 — Graham's mercurial pendulum was put into use.

1726 — Ebenezer Parmelee of Guilford, Connecticut, built a clock that was installed in the town's church tower.

1727 — John Harrison's gridiron pendulum was put into use.

1730 — The German clock maker Anton Ketterer made his first cuckoo clock.

1738-1770 — In Lancaster, Pennsylvania, Abraham LeRoy made quality tall case clocks with brass dials. In colonial days, a few women were clock makers. One of them, Anna Maria LeRoy, the daughter of Abraham LeRoy, had the opportunity to watch her father at work and later produced clocks. She married Wilmer Atkinson in 1749. The dials of her clocks from 1750 to 1760 bore his name.

1740 — The first cuckoo clocks were made in the Black Forest region of Germany, but it took several decades before this style of clock became popular.

After 1740 — Mahogany was used for British clock cases.

1750 — Round dials were introduced for shelf clocks. Edward Duffield made Philadelphia's first town clock.

1749-1796 — The most noted clock maker from the Philadelphia area was David Rittenhouse. In the years before the Revolutionary War, he inherited some books and tools from his uncle, which may have aroused his interest in mechanics. He began making high quality clocks in 1749. After the former English colonies became the United States of America, Rittenhouse came to know and work with American leaders including Benjamin Franklin and Thomas Jefferson. He made astronomical instruments and started the first observatory in the United States. He was recognized as a scientist as well as a maker of quality clocks.

1759   Lever escapement was invented by Thomas Mudge of London.

1760   The four Willard brothers from Grafton, Massachusetts, were clock makers. The first one to take up this trade, around 1760, was Benjamin who worked in various places including Grafton.
            A clock maker was able to produce between 12 and 20 tall clocks a year. A hundred years later the output of shelf clocks would be in the 150,000 range. This great increase was due to the development and use of mass production methods.

1765   The compensation balance was first made by Pierre Le Roy of Paris.

1770   David Rittenhouse set up a clock shop in Philadelphia. Tall case clocks with brass works were his specialty.

1772-1852   Eli Terry was considered the "father" of the clock making industry.

Pre 1775   In colonial America, craftsmen made clocks to order, one at a time. This was an expensive process. Brass movements were fashioned by hand with simple tools. Boston, New York and Philadelphia were all centers for the production of the tall-case floor clocks, better known as grandfather clocks. During this time, there were several hundred clock makers at work in the colonies.

1775-1783   Clock making in the colonies came to a halt during the Revolutionary War as clock makers joined the fighting forces or made equipment for the soldiers. Many clock makers became gunsmiths.

Circa 1789 Amos Jewett (1753-1834), a clock maker in New Lebanon, New York, made wooden tall clocks with printed paper dials. He numbered and dated his clocks so one knows that clock 12 was made in 1789 whereas clock 38 was a 1796 product.

1790 to 1812 Gideon Roberts, a Revolutionary War veteran, possibly was the first to use mass production methods in his Bristol, Connecticut, clock factory where both hanging wall clocks and tall-case clocks were made. Many were sold to out-of-state buyers. Since brass clock works were expensive, he created his own wooden movements and used printed paper dials. Some clocks were made without cases. Since the pendulum could be seen easily as it swung back and forth, the descriptive phrase "wag on the wall" became an appropriate name for these caseless clocks. Of course, a buyer could make a case or have a wood worker fashion one and then he would own a conventional clock. Roberts assembled his 30-hour tall-case clocks with their wooden movements in groups of 10 or more at a time. This innovation speeded up the production process and made less costly clocks available to buyers.

1792-1795   David Rittenhouse served as the director of the U.S. mint in Philadelphia.

1793   Following the completion of his apprenticeship, Eli Terry began making clocks near Plymouth, Connecticut.

Nov. 1797   Eli Terry was awarded a patent for an "equation clock" which had 2 dials. One dial showed sun time and the other true time.

1800s

Circa 1800 The production of wooden clocks began in the United States.

After 1800 Gideon Roberts owned an assembly plant in Richmond, Virginia. Eli Terry learned how to use water power to drive machinery. This helped to increase the production of clock parts.

1802-1840   Simon Willard made about 4,000 clocks during this time span. One was the banjo clock which sold for $35. Early 19th century clock making was a problem because metal was scarce and the supply of glass was limited.
            Everything had to be done by hand and the craftsman and his apprentice used the simplest tools in their work: a hammer, drill and file.

1802-1860   Banjo clocks were made in the United States.

1802   Simon Willard patented his "Improved Timepiece," later called "banjo" because of its shape. Originally, most examples were time only. This popular clock style has been copied consistently over the years. Eli Terry's first factory established.

1806   Eli Terry was making about 200 clocks a year.

1807-1809   The Jefferson Embargo limited the importation of material from English factories.

1807-1810   Eli Terry contracted to make an unheard of 4,000 hang-up clock movements at $4 each in three years' time. The water power-driven machines he designed produced identical interchangeable wooden parts for inexpensive (grandfather type) clock works. Silas Hoadley and Seth Thomas worked for him. Terry is credited with introducing the factory system of mass production. This helped start the factory system in the United States. Inexpensive clocks, made in quantities, became available to the public.

1809-1810   Eli Terry established a partnership with Seth Thomas.

1810-1813   Seth Thomas and Silas Hoadley bought Eli Terry's Plymouth clock shop. Thomas sold out in 1813 and Hoadley continued in business.

1812   Eli Terry set up an experimental shop that produced low-priced wooden shelf clocks.

1811-1830s Six Ives brothers, including Joseph and Chauncey, were involved in the clock industry.

1813   Seth Thomas set up his own shop in Plymouth Hollow, Connecticut, where he became a prolific clock maker.

1816   Eli Terry patented a pillar-and-scroll shelf clock with a 30-hour wooden works that evolved from his plain box-type case. This clock cost about fifteen dollars and ran 30 hours on a single winding. For a short time, Chauncey Jerome made clock cases for Eli Terry.

Circa 1818   Joseph Ives made a brass clock movement with steel plates. An agreement was reached between Seth Thomas and Eli Terry that stated Thomas was to pay Terry a royalty of 50 cents for each clock made. Sales under this agreement produced about 5,000 clock movements.

August 1817   Joseph Ives (1782-1862) applied for a patent for looking-glass clock cases.

July 1819   The firm of Joseph Ives and Company was dissolved.

1819-1822   Large numbers of wall mirror clocks were made by Birge and his associates.

1820   The manufacture of side-column clocks began.

1820-1830   Circumventing Terry's patent, other companies varied the pillar-and-scroll clock, frequently using brass eight-day movements,

1820-1840   Most of the Connecticut clock industry produced wooden shelf clocks. These clocks sold for less than $10. Brass clocks, on the other hand, ranged in price from $15 to $33 or more.

1822   Joseph Ives of Bristol patented a looking-glass clock, but Aaron Willard claimed that Massachusetts makers had been using looking glasses to add variety to clock fronts for some 25 years.

Circa 1822   The "Lighthouse" clock was patterned after the Eddystone Lighthouse at Plymouth, one of the earliest in England. This clock was introduced by Simon Willard. It was eight-day, weight driven and had an alarm. A glass dome covered the clock.

1822-1855   Birge was associated with the clock makers Ives, Case, Gilbert, Fuller and Peck.

1824   Chauncey Jerome formed a partnership with his brother, Noble, and Elijah Darrow for the manufacture of clocks. The firm was called Jeromes & Darrow, and was the largest producer of clocks at the time.

Joseph Ives perfected a spring driven shelf clock using flat leafed springs instead of coiled ones.

Circa 1825   Jerome patented a "bronze looking glass clock" with a 30-hour wooden movement, using a mirror instead of a tablet and bronze-colored pilasters. Jerome specialized in case building and usually bought his movements from others.

Joseph Ives had learned how to make rolled brass. He moved to Brooklyn, New York, where he stayed briefly and invented the wagon spring to power a clock. The wagon spring is a series of flat-leafed arched springs that resemble those used in wagons.

1825-1920   "OG" or "ogee," S-curved, veneer-framed clocks were made and sold widely throughout this 95-year period. They were prolonged best sellers.

1827   Chauncey Jerome invented a one-day weight driven clock named the OG which sold for one

dollar. Over one half million sold in a single year.

1828   Elias Ingraham settled in Bristol as a cabinet and case maker of clocks.

Mark Leavenworth of Waterbury, Connecticut, made wooden movements for clocks.

After 1829   Samuel Terry (1774-1853) became an important producer of wooden movements in Bristol, Connecticut. Marsh, Gilbert & Company operated a clock business in Bristol.

1830   Eli Terry's son, Silas B. Terry, patented a method for tempering coiled springs so they could be produced inexpensively.

Irenus Atkins, a Baptist minister, started a clock factory in Bristol, converting a church into a factory, as no other building was available for his purpose.

The spring balance was invented.

After 1830   Rolled brass became more available for clock movements. Chauncey Jerome gave his brother, Noble, an idea for replacing wooden clock works with inexpensive rolled-brass movements. Some authorities feel that Chauncey copied Joseph Ives' mirror clock and his brass movement.

1831   Elias Ingraham founded the E. Ingraham Company. Terrysville Post Office was established on Dec. 22, 1831, in honor of Eli Terry.

J. C. Brown made clocks in Bristol, Connecticut.

Circa 1832   Daniel Pratt, Jr., was a clock maker in Reading, Massachusetts.

1831-1837   Burr & Chittenden were making clocks in Lexington, Massachusetts.

1832-1836   Boardman and Wells made a large number of wooden-movement shelf clocks, using the facilities of four factories for their manufacture.

1833   Elisha Brewster started a factory at Bristol, which came to be known as Brewster & Ingraham.

Eli Terry retired from active clock making.

1836   James S. Ives of Bristol received a patent for a brass coiled clock spring.

1837-1843   The firm of Birge & Mallory experienced prosperous times due to the manufacture and sales of clocks.

1838   The brass shelf clock was developed.

Circa 1840s   Elias Ingraham, Bristol, designed a sharp Gothic clock popularly called a "Steeple" clock.

1840   Spring driven clocks were introduced.

The largest clock factory was the Jerome Company owned by Chauncey Jerome.

1840-1842   Jerome sent a shipment of his brass clocks to England. The English authorities bought the entire lot. He sent another lot and they bought all of these, too. When the first shipment arrived, the English buyers realized that a really inexpensive and reliable clock was being imported and they allowed them to be sold.

1840-1850   All American clocks were weight driven until the Mid 19th century because the United States did not have rolling mills that were capable of producing spring steel.

1842-1849	J. C. Brown became J. C. Brown & Company and also used the name Forestville Manufacturing Company. This period marked the partnership years of Edward Howard and David P. Davis whose principal product was the banjo clock.
1843	The partnership of Boardman & Wells ended and Wells and other clock makers formed the Bristol Company.
1844	John Birge and Thomas Fuller formed a partnership that lasted until the death of Fuller in 1848. Brothers Elias and Andrew Ingraham formed a partnership with Elisha C. Brewster and started producing the steeple clock which rapidly gained in popularity. This innovation soon replaced the large three-section Empire case, known as a "triple-decker," which was a popular item among Connecticut clock makers of the 1830s. Chauncey Jerome had 12 brass clock factories in Bristol and a case factory in New Haven, Connecticut.
1845	When one of Jerome's Bristol factories burned down, 50,000 to 75,000 brass movements were destroyed. By this year clocks were made in Connecticut at the rate of nearly a million a year.
1846	Jerome moved his entire operation from Bristol to New Haven, Connecticut.
1847	An economic depression stopped American clock making and was the end of the wooden clock movement.
1848	A Howard tower clock was installed in a church in New Hampshire.
1849	American Clock Company, New York City, was organized as a large depository to sell clocks made by various clock makers. The company issued a catalog showing the clocks that were for sale.
1850	Weight driven clocks were gradually replaced by spring driven ones. The Ansonia Clock Company was established in Ansonia, Connecticut, by Anson Phelps.
Circa 1850	Brass-coiled springs were largely replaced by better and cheaper steel springs. Nicholas Muller was at work in a foundry in New York City where he made iron-front clocks. Chauncey Jerome built America's largest manufacturing concern for clocks.
1850-1860	The production of tall clocks came to a stand still.
1851	Samuel Emerson Root was at work in Bristol where he made some marine-type movements.
Circa 1851	The William L. Gilbert Clock Company, Plymouth, was incorporated. Hiram Camp started the New Haven Clock Company in New Haven. John H. Hawes of Ithaca, New York, patented the first known simple-mechanism calendar clock.
After 1853	Many patents were issued for calendar clocks.
1853-1959	The New Haven Clock Company was in business.
1853-now	The Seth Thomas Clock Company was in business.
	ness.
1854	A fire at the Ansonia Clock Company forced the company to move to Phelp's Mill under the new name of Ansonia Brass and Copper Company.
1855	The New Haven Clock Company took over Jerome Manufacturing Company but continued to use the Jerome name. John Briggs of Concord, New Hampshire, received a patent for a clock escapement called "Briggs Rotary." The Ansonia Bobbing doll was patented. The E & A Ingraham clock plant in Bristol burned. Through financial reverses, Chauncey Jerome went bankrupt.
1855-1900+	In this time period calendar clocks were a popular commodity in this country.
1857	The Waterbury Clock Company was in business. Solomon Spring owned a clock company.
1859	The Ansonia Swinging doll was patented. Seth Thomas died. Westminster chimes were introduced.
Circa 1863	F. Kroeber manufactured clocks in New York City, made fine cases and often altered purchased movements.
1863-1868	L. F. and W. W. Carter made calendar clocks.
1864	Mozart, Beach & Hubbell patented a perpetual-calendar clock that needed to be wound only once a year. E. N. Welch of Bristol consolidated the clock companies he purchased under the name of E. N. Welch Manufacturing Company.
1865	When the Ithaca Calendar Clock Company was established, it used Henry B. Horton's perpetual roller-type calendar clock patent. The American clock industry exported over nine hundred thousand dollars worth of clocks to over 30 countries.
1866	Plymouth Hollow became Thomaston, Connecticut, to honor the Seth Thomas name. As a result, clock labels were changed to "Thomaston."
1866-1964	The William L. Gilbert Clock Company was in business.
1867	A battery-operated clock was marketed. Alfonso Broadman, Forestville, Connecticut, made a simple calendar clock with two rollers, one for the month and the date and the other for the day of the week.
1868	The Welch, Spring & Company partnership was organized, specializing in the manufacture of regulator and calendar clocks. Joseph K. Seem's patent showed the way to attach three small disks to the back of an existing clock dial, making it a simple calendar clock.
1868-1893	Parker & Whipple Clock Company operated in Meriden, Connecticut.
1869	Celluloid, a flammable plastic, was developed. It was later used on clock cases to simulate tortoise shell, amber, onyx and other materials.
1870s-1880	George Owen, Winsted, Connecticut, had a

small shop that later merged with Gilbert and Company.

1871   Daniel Gale, Sheboygan Wisconsin, patented an astronomical calendar clock dial.

1872   Terrysville, Connecticut became Terryville. Joseph K. Seem obtained a patent for a perpetual calendar roller mechanism that could be fitted on top of an existing clock when space permitted.

1878 or before   Ansonia clocks were marked "Ansonia, Connecticut."

1878 or later   Ansonia clocks were marked "New York."

1879   Ansonia Clock Company moved to Brooklyn, New York. Shortly after the move, a fire destroyed the factory.

Circa 1880   Nicholas Muller's Sons made fancy shelf-clock cases of iron and bronze. A song that gave a name for the long-case clock said, "My grandfather clock was too tall for the shelf, so it stood ninety years on the floor."

1880   H. J. Davis made an illuminated alarm clock.

1881   Joseph K. Seem was granted a patent that improved his original 1872 perpetual calendar mechanism.

1882   The Macomb Calendar Clock Company was formed in Illinois. The company used Seem's 1881 calendar clock patent.

1881-1885   Yale Clock Company, New Haven, Connecticut advertised novelty clocks.

1883   The Macomb Calendar Clock Company went out of business.

A. D. Clausen patented the "Ignatz" (flying pendulum) clock.

Benjamin Franklin, Chicago, patented a perpetual calendar clock mechanism that could be attached to an existing clock by cutting a hole in its dial.

1885   The Sidney Advertising Clock Company, Sydney, New York, developed a large wall clock on which advertising drums turned every five minutes.

Dec. 23 1885   The United Clock Company was formed and made about 50 alarm clocks a day. However, the company only lasted 2 years before going bankrupt.

1886-1916   Darche Electric Clock Company, Chicago and Jersey City, New Jersey, made battery-alarm timepieces.

Circa 1888   The Self Winding Clock Company, New York City and Brooklyn, made battery-powered and electric clocks.

1888   The F. Kroeber Clock Co. catalogue showed a selection of 15 eight day walnut shelf or mantel clocks with gong strike named Fulton, Angel Swing No. 2, Corinth, Congress, Mariposa, Leghorn, Jefferson, Floretta, Essex, Virgil, Wanderer, Vixen, Thunderer, Polaris, Artic and Langtry.

1890   Edward P. Baird & Company was established in Plattsburgh, New York. It used the Seth Thomas works and papier-mâché for the body.

Circa 1890   Jenning Brothers Manufacturing Company of Bridgeport, Connecticut, made metal clocks.

1891-1897   Henry Prentiss of New York City received various patents for calendar mechanisms that ran for one year after being wound.

1893   The Parker Clock Co., Meriden, Connecticut, took over Parker & Whipple. The firm made small pendulum desk clocks, round alarm clocks and novelty clocks.

1895   Western Clock Manufacturing Company began in La Salle, Illinois.

1896-1900   Edward P. Baird & Company moved to Evanston, Illinois, where it made wooden-case clocks with metal dials trimmed with embossed and painted advertisements.

1897   Chelsea Clock Company operated in Chelsea, Massachusetts. The company's output included auto and ship clocks, as well as those for the home.

Late 1800s   Simplex Company of Gardner, Massachusetts, made time recorders and time clocks.

Decalcomania transfers were common on clock tablets.

1900s

1902   John P. Peatfield of Arlington, Massachusetts, patented a perpetual calendar clock with a spring driven mechanism that was wound yearly.

1903   Sessions Clock Company, Bristol-Forestville, Connecticut, bought E. N. Welch Manufacturing Company.

1903-1968   The Sessions Clock Company was in business.

1908   The Loheide Mfg. Co. made a black-case metal-trimmed shelf clock that contained a slot-machine arrangement that took $2.50 gold pieces. The patent number 883,886 dates the clock to 1908.

1910   "Big Ben" alarm clocks were made.

1915   "Little Ben" alarm clocks were made.

Circa 1917   Paul Lux of Waterbury, Connecticut, founded the Lux Clock Manufacturing Company and produced many novelty clocks. He used molded wood cases.

1929   International Business Machine Corporation (IBM), Endicott, New York, was organized.

Ansonia Clock Company's equipment and materials were purchased by the Soviet government and moved to the Soviet Union.

1931   August C. Keebler of Chicago founded the August C. Keebler Company, which marketed Lux Clocks, including the pendulettes that he sold to large mail-order companies. He did not make clocks, but his name was sometimes used on Lux Clocks.

Westclox, a trade name, became the new name for Western Clock Manufacturing Company.

Hammond Clock Company was in operation.

Elisha Hotchkiss mahogany mirror shelf clock, dated 1835, 30-hour, time and strike, weight driven with wooden dial and movement, top repainted but all original. Mirror clocks were very popular during the first half of the nineteenth century. $350.

Chauncey Jerome invented the case and movement of OG clocks. Shown here is one of his mahogany OG clocks with brass dial, circa 1845, 30-hour, time and strike, 15-1/2" wide, 26" high; $300.

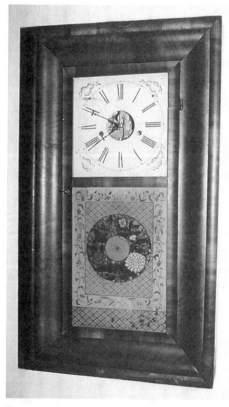

Seth Thomas mahogany veneered shelf clock with artificially grained pillars, circa 1855-59, eight-day, time and strike, weight driven; 16-1/2" wide, 32-1/2" high; $400.

Forestville Manufacturing Company, mahogany OG, circa 1855, with maker J. C. Brown on the label, eight-day, time and strike, weight driven, 16" wide, 29" high; $350.

W. L. Gilbert mahogany OG, eight-day, time and strike, weight driven, 15-1/2" wide, 26" high; $250.

New Haven miniature rosewood steeple clock with reverse painting on tablet; 30-hour, time and strike, spring driven; 7-1/2" wide, 14-1/2" high; $200.

Ansonia "Bobbing Doll" (moves up and down as pendulum) metal shelf clock, patented December 14, 1886, 30-hour time only, spring driven; 14-1/2" high; $1,600.

L. F. & W. W. Carter rosewood double-dial perpetual calendar, top dial records days and bottom dial records months and dates, eight-day, time and strike, 13-1/2" wide, 21" high; $600.

F. Kroeber cast-iron black enameled mantel clock, circa 1898, gilded decorations, eight-day, time and strike, 12-1/2" high; $275.

E. N. Welch mahogany miniature OG, 30-hour, time and strike, original dial and tablet, 12" wide, 19" high; $225.

Celluloid was invented in 1869 but was not widely used until the end of the century. Shown here is a Lux Clock Company miniature celluloid mantel clock, 8" wide, 4-1/2" high; $45.

Self Winding Clock Company, battery-operated oak wall clock; time only; 19-1/2" wide, 30" high, 7" dial; $450.

Macomb Calendar Clock Company, walnut perpetual calendar clock, circa 1882-1883, incised carving, moon phases on lower dial, eight-day, time and strike, 13" wide, 28" high; $4,800.

Western Clock Manufacturing Company, La Salle, Illinois, brass finished iron front shelf clock with female figure holding up the clock, 30-hour, time only, 6-1/2" wide, 12" high; $175.

Lux cuckoo pendulette, molded wood, bird sitting on the top, 30-hour, time only, spring driven, 4" wide, 6-1/2" high; $45.

Chapter 3

Representative Clocks from Smaller Clockmakers

Most of the following companies or individual clock makers produced clocks in small quantities and they are not as prevalent on the market as the products of the major companies. For this reason, we have put them together in this chapter to highlight the contributions made by these tradesmen. In most cases, their clocks will be found among those from the early 19th century when a great deal of experimentation was being done in an attempt to produce better and more efficient clocks.

Clocks manufactured by the major clock companies include Ansonia Clock Company, the E. Ingraham Company, E.N. Welch Manufacturing Company, Eli Terry, William L. Gilbert Clock Company, New Haven Clock Company, Seth Thomas, and the Waterbury Clock Company. Examples of their timepieces will be pictured in the sections covering the various types of clocks.

Mitchell, Atkins & Company, Bristol, Connecticut, mahogany veneered mirror shelf clock with artificially grained columns and gold stenciling above dial, circa 1830-36; 30-hour, time, strike, and alarm, weight driven; 16-1/2" wide, 32" high; $500.

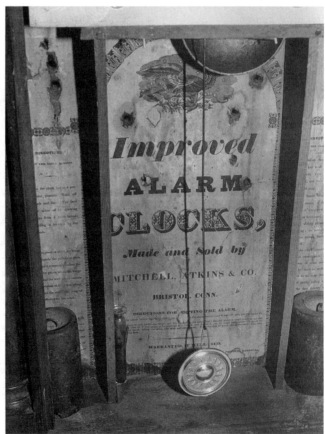

Label from Mitchell, Atkins & Company mirror shelf clock.

Ball Watch Company, Cleveland, oak octagon, short-drop wall clock, circa 1880, eight-day, time only, spring driven; 24" high, 12" dial; $400.

Baird Advertiser, Plattsburgh, New York, papier-mâché case wall clock, with movement by Seth Thomas, circa 1890; eight-day, time only, spring driven; 18-1/2" wide, 30-1/2" high; $1,500.

Label from E.M. Barnes transition shelf clock with old wooden movement. Label reads, "Improved clocks manufactured and sold by E.M. Barnes, Bristol, Conn. At wholesale and retail. Warranted if well used."

Birge & Mallory mahogany beehive shelf clock with a J. Ives patented movement, circa 1838-43; eight-day, time and strike, wagon spring driven; 14" wide, 26-1/2" high; $2,500.

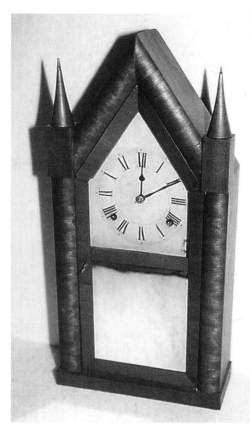

*Chauncey Boardman mahogany veneer mirror tablet stee-
ple clock, circa 1845, 30-hour, reverse fusee movement,
time and strike, 10" wide, 20" high; $400.*

*W. Boardman mahogany wall clock, circa 1825, with
wooden works, stenciled splat and column case, tablet is
not original, 16-1/2" wide, 31-1/2" high; $325.*

*Brewster & Ingraham rosewood veneer double OG wall clock,
circa 1840; 30-hour, time only, 15" wide, 25-1/2" high; $300.*

*J. C. Brown rosewood steeple clock, time and strike, circa
1850, 10" wide, 19-1/2" high; $400.*

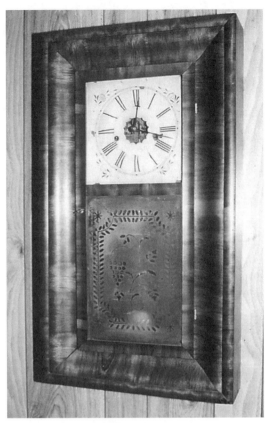

J.C. Brown rosewood double OG, circa 1855, original tablet, eight-day, time and strike, 16-1/2" wide, 29" high; $350.

J.C. Brown & Company rosewood steeple clock, circa 1842-49; eight-day, time and strike, spring driven; 10" wide, 20" high; $500.

Burroughs Clock Company, Lowell, Massachusetts, mahogany veneered, miniature steeple clock, circa 1870-74; 4-3/4" wide, 7" high; $125.

L.F. & W. W. Carter, Bristol, Connecticut, rosewood perpetual calendar clock with double dial, circa 1863-68; eight-day, time only, weight driven; 22" wide, 59" high, top dial 17-1/2", bottom dial 11-1/2"; $2,500.

Chelsea "Number 1" oak round top, long-drop regulator, circa 1897; eight-day, time only, weight driven; 10-1/2" wide, 32" high, 12" dial; $1,250.

Chelsea walnut banjo clock, circa 1890, time only with single weight driven, made in Boston, 39" high; $3,500.

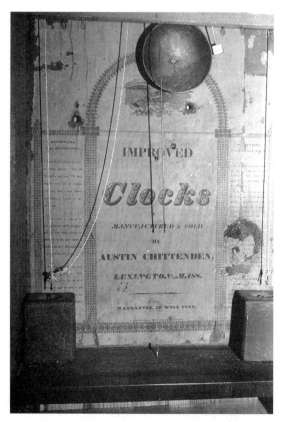

Austin Chittenden rosewood, mirror shelf clock, wooden works, circa 1831-37; 30-hour, time, strike, and alarm, weight driven; 16" wide, 41" high; $1,000.

Label from Austin Chittenden mirror shelf clock.

Forestville Manufacturing Company, also called J.C. Brown, mahogany transition wall clock with gilded columns, eight-day, time and strike, weight driven, 18" wide, 35" high; $500.

Hopkins & Alfred Clock Co. mahogany mirror shelf clock, circa 1825, wooden works, weight driven, time and strike, 17" wide, 30-1/2" high; $425.

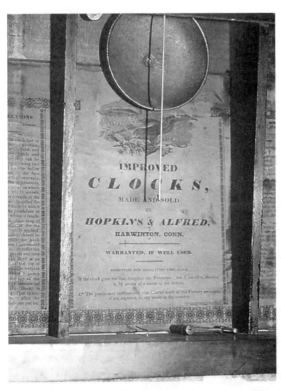

Label from Hopkins & Alfred mirror shelf clock. The label reads, "Improved clocks, made and sold by Hopkins & Alfred Clock Co., Harwinton, Conn. Warranted if well used."

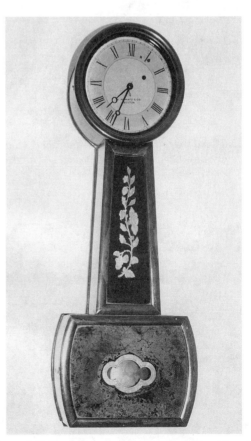

E. Howard & Company rosewood rounded end box banjo wall clock, circa 1840; eight-day, time only; 11" wide at base, 28-1/2" high, 7" dial; $1,800.

C. & L.C. Ives triple-decker mahogany, circa 1835, shelf clock with side pillars and ball feet, 18" wide, 38" high; $700.

L. Hubel bird's eye maple advertising shelf clock, circa 1870, eight-day, time only, 10-1/2" wide, 24" high; $2,500.

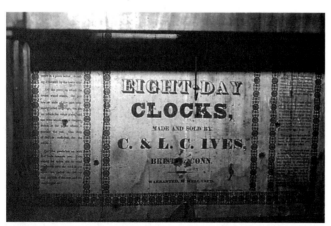

Label from C. & L.C. Ives triple-decker shelf clock. It reads, "Eight-day clocks, made and sold by C. & L.C. Ives, Bristol, Conn. Warranted if well used."

Wooden dial to C. & L.C. Ives triple-decker shelf clock. Notice the opening above the center which allows one to see the movement.

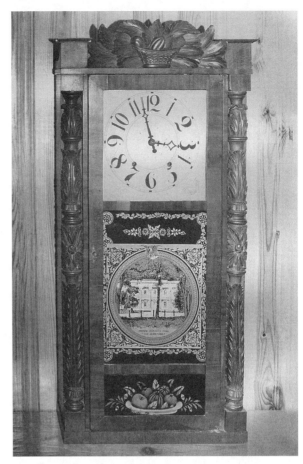

Brass strap movement from C. & L.C. Ives triple-decker shelf clock.

Ives style Empire mahogany shelf clock, early 1800s; eight-day, time and strike, weight driven, brass strap movement; 18" wide, 35-1/2" high; $550.

Jerome oak double-dial perpetual calendar shelf clock, circa 1850; an exact copy of case and calendar movement; eight-day, time and strike, spring driven; 10-1/2" wide, 21-1/2" high, 3-1/2" top dial, 4-1/2" bottom dial; $1,000 for exact copy, $1,500 for original.

Jerome & Co. papier-mâché shelf clock with mother-of-pearl inlay and fusee movement, eight-day, time and strike, 11" wide, 14" high; $950.

Label from Jerome & Co. transition shelf clock. It reads, in part, "Thirty hour clocks, with extra bushed movements, manufactured by Jerome & Co., New Haven, Conn. Instructions for setting the clock running and keeping it in order."

Jerome & Co. rosewood transition shelf clock with half columns, circa 1851, 30-hour time and strike, weight driven, 15" wide, 25" high; $250.

Partial label from Jerome & Co. mahogany shelf clock.

E. Ingraham oak kitchenette shelf clock, circa 1930, eight day, time and strike, 13-1/2" wide, 13-1/2" high, $150

Chauncey Jerome mahogany miniature round band OG, circa 1868, eight-day, time, strike and alarm, tablet not original, 11" wide, 16-1/2" high; $350.

Chauncey Jerome rosewood veneer OG mirror wall clock, 30-hour, time and strike, circa 1848, 15" wide, 25-1/2" high; $250.

Label from a Chauncey Jerome OG shelf clock. It reads, in part, "Patent brass clocks, manufactured and sold by Chauncey Jerome, New Haven, Conn. Warranted good. Directions for setting the clock running and keeping it in order..."

Jerome, Darrow & Company rosewood shelf clock, wooden works, with President Jackson's Hermitage on tablet, circa 1825; eight-day, time and strike, weight driven; 19" wide, 40" high; $900.

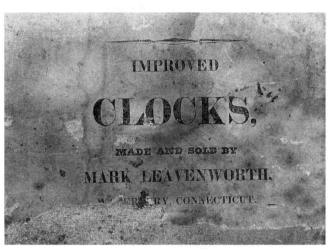

Label from Mark Leavenworth pillar and scroll shelf clock.

Mark Leavenworth mahogany veneered and stained hardwoods pillar and scroll shelf clock, replaced brass finials, ivory escutcheon, circa 1825; 30-hour, time and strike, weight driven; 16-1/2" wide, 31" high; $3,500.

Macomb Calendar Clock Company "Kokomo" (left) walnut calendar shelf clock, circa 1882-83; eight-day, time and strike, spring driven; 16-1/2" wide, 28" high, 6" dial; $4,000. Macomb Calendar Clock Company walnut calendar shelf clock, circa 1882-83; eight-day, time and strike, spring driven; 15-1/2" wide, 28" high, 6" dial; $4,000. Both clocks have original cases but with new moon dial and missing calendars at base.

Elisha Manross mahogany double OG, circa 1845, 30-hour, time and strike, 15-1/2" wide, 26" high; $300.

Label from Elisha Manross OG shelf clock. It reads, "Thirty hour clocks, warranted good. Made and sold by Elisha Manross, Bristol, Conn."

Elisha Manross mahogany OG shelf clock, 30-hour, time and strike, circa 1848, 15-1/2" wide, 43" high; $300.

Label from Elisha Manross OG shelf clock. It reads, in part, "Patent thirty hour brass clocks, made and sold by Elisha Manross, Bristol, Conn. Warranted good. Directions for setting the clock running and keeping it in order..."

Marsh, Gilbert & Company mahogany veneered shelf clock, wooden works, circa 1830; 30-hour, time and strike, weight driven; 17-1/2" wide, 32-1/2" high; $375.

Label from Marsh, Gilbert & Company mahogany veneered shelf clock.

Close-up of mechanism showing wooden works in Marsh, Gilbert & Company mahogany veneered shelf clock.

George B. Owen Clock Company, New York, walnut wall clock, circa 1854; eight-day, time and bell strike; 13" wide, 36" high, 7-1/2" dial; $750.

Orton, Preston, & Co. mahogany shelf clock, circa 1828-1835, with side columns, wooden movement, 30-hour, single weight, 16-1/2" wide, 31-1/2" high; $395.

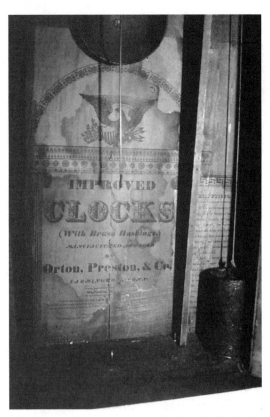

Parker Clock Company, Meriden, Connecticut, solid brass, wooden base barrel shelf clock, circa 1870; eight-day, time and strike, double barrel spring driven; 14" wide, 8-1/2" deep, 10-1/2" high; $1,600.

Label from Orton, Preston, & Co. shelf clock. It reads, "Improved clocks (with brass bushings) manufactured and sold by Orton, Preston, & Co., Farmington, Conn."

Parker Clock Company, miniature brass simple calendar shelf clock, patented March 14, 1882; 30-hour, time only, spring driven; 5" wide, 8-1/2" high; $750.

The Prentiss Clock Company, New York, mahogany calendar clock, circa 1890; 60-day, time only, double spring movement and spring driven calendar that only needs to be wound once a year; 12" wide, 36" high, 9-1/2" dial; $2,500.

Roswell-Kimberly rosewood shelf clock, 1850-1860, with top finials and columns, eight-day, time and strike, 11" wide, 21" high; $500.

Russell and Jones walnut parlor clock, incised carving, eight-day, time, strike and alarm, 14" wide, 22-1/2" high; $350.

Sidney Advertiser, Sidney, New York, oak calendar wall clock, with movement by Seth Thomas; repainted tablet and replaced exact copies of advertising drums; eight-day, time only, spring driven; 28" wide, 72" high; $9,000.

Southern Calendar Clock Co. mahogany "Fashion Number 2," calendar clock, eight-day, time and strike, Pat. July 4. 1876. The cases and the time movements were made by Seth Thomas and the calendar mechanism used was the Andrews Calendar patent. The company was located in St. Louis, Missouri; $1,500.

Elmer Stennes mahogany ribbon stripe banjo clock, marked MCIP (made clock in prison), one weight, time only, 7" dial, 44" high; $2,750.

E. Terry & Sons rosewood pillar and scroll shelf clock, wooden works, circa 1818-24; 30-hour, time and strike, weight driven; 17-1/2" wide, 31" high; $1,250.

Eli Terry rosewood mirror shelf clock with carved columns and eagle splat, wooden works, circa 1827; 30-hour, time and strike, weight driven; 20" wide, 37" high; $1,000.

Label from E. Terry & Sons pillar and scroll shelf clock.

Eli Terry & Son mahogany shelf clock, wooden works, 1825-36; 30-hour, time and strike, weight driven; 17-1/2" wide, 31" high; $1,500.

Label from Eli Terry & Son mahogany shelf clock.

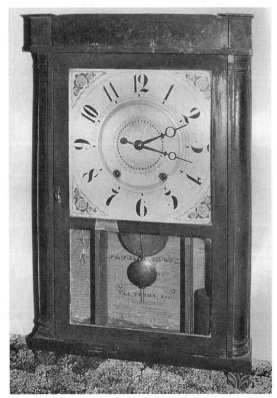

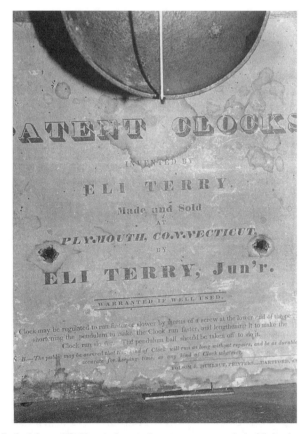

Eli Terry, Jr., mahogany veneered shelf clock, wooden works, circa 1834-37; 30-hour, time and strike, weight driven; 16-3/4" wide, 26" high; $800.

Label from Eli Terry, Jr., mahogany veneered shelf clock.

Samuel Terry, Bristol, Connecticut, mahogany veneered mirror shelf clock, with artificially grained columns and ivory escutcheon, circa 1829; 30-hour, time and strike, weight driven; 17" wide, 34" high; $400.

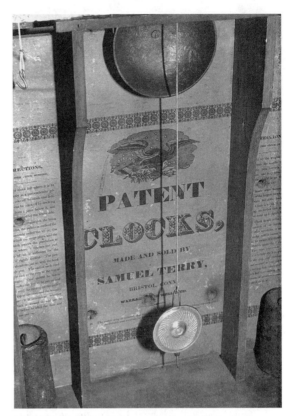

Label from Samuel Terry mirror shelf clock.

Seth Thomas, Plymouth Hollow, Connecticut, mahogany veneered shelf clock with ebony and gold-leaf painted columns; 30-hour, time and strike, weight driven, brass movement patented 1867 (may not be the original movement); 18-1/2" wide, 32-1/2" high; $600.

Terry Clock Company walnut octagon short-drop simple calendar clock, eight-day, time only, spring driven; 14-1/2" wide, 22-1/2" high, 9" dial; $350.

Welch, Spring & Co. rosewood calendar clock with B.B. Lewis's perpetual movement, patented Dec. 18, 1868, eight-day, time and strike, 11" wide, 20" high; $1,050.

M. Welton mahogany, mirror door OG shelf clock, circa 1845, repainted dial Welton made both clocks and cases, 30-hour, time and strike, 16" wide, 26" high; $300.

M. Welton label on OG shelf clock. It reads, in part, "M. Welton's improved clokes, 54 John Street, New York. Warranted." "Clocks" is spelled as "clokes" on the label.

William. M. Wrigley Clock Company, "Chicago" marked on movement, oak octagon, short-drop simple calendar clock; eight-day, time only, spring driven; 17" wide, 24" high; $475.

Chapter 4

Leading Clock Makers

Ansonia Clock Company

Anson G. Phelps, a wealthy Connecticut importer of tin, brass, and copper, founded the Ansonia Clock Company in 1850. This was six years after he had built a copper rolling mill near Derby, Connecticut, at a place he called Ansonia.

Phelps started the business with a capital of $100,000. His associates in this enterprise were Eli Terry and Franklin C. Andrews. Their firm was advertised in the Connecticut Business Directory with the following declaration: "Ansonia Clock Company, Manufacturers and Dealers in Clocks and Timepieces of every description, Wholesale and Retail, Ansonia, Connecticut."

After a fire destroyed the factory in 1854, Phelps' company moved to Ansonia where it was renamed the Ansonia Brass and Copper Company. At this location, the company made clocks from 1864 to 1878. The Ansonia Clock Company was again organized in 1878 after moving its clock making operations to Brooklyn, New York. Shortly after this move, in the late 1880s, a fire destroyed the factory. A year later, after the completion of the new factory in Brooklyn, their business expanded. Many new styles of clocks were made and novelty and figurine clocks became a big part of their clock making enterprise.

All sorts of wall and shelf clocks, including swing clocks, were introduced. Imitation French clocks, as well as novelties, such as the "Bobbing Doll" and "Swinging Doll," patented in 1855 and 1859 respectively, were marketed. An 1889 catalog showing Ansonia clocks featured three versions of the Bobbers, called Jumper No. 1, Jumper No. 2 and Jumper No. 3. Ansonia was known for its diversity of clock types; many of the older and unusual ones have been reproduced, including the previously mentioned "Bobbing" and "Swinging" dolls.

The company's specialty clocks included the Swing clocks, in which female figures held the swinging pendulums. Also popular were the Royal Bonn porcelain shelf varieties and the statue clocks, which the company advertised as figure clocks. Among its novelty clocks, the Crystal Palace, Sonnet, Helmsmen, and Army and Navy have proved to be excellent collector's items and have rapidly increased in value. The clocks were marked "New York" as their place of origin.

Just prior to World War 1, Ansonia had sales representatives in Australia, New Zealand, Japan, China, and India, as well as a score of other countries. After the conclusion of this war, its business deteriorated in quality and dropped measurably in the number of clocks produced. Manufacturing stopped in the spring of 1929. By the end of that year, the company's material assets were sold to the Russian government. Sad as it was to accept, this great clock manufacturing company, creative as any other American clock company, was defunct after the summer of 1929.

William L. Gilbert Clock Company

George Marsh and William L. Gilbert purchased a clock shop in 1828 which they named Marsh, Gilbert & Company. They were soon at work in two Connecticut cities, Bristol and Farmington.

In 1837, John Birge joined William Lewis Gilbert and the company name became Birge, Gilbert & Company. They made Empire-style shelf clocks.

The company name continued to change. From 1839-1840 Jerome, Grant, Gilbert & Company was established. Clock makers Chauncey and Noble Jerome and Zelotas Grant went into partnership with Gilbert to create Jerome's inexpensive brass movement clocks.

In 1841, Gilbert and Lucius Clarke acquired a clock factory in Winsted, Connecticut. Later the town name was changed to Winchester. Ezra Baldwin was a member of this company for a time.

From 1841-1845 Clarke, Gilbert & Company produced inexpensive brass clocks. In 1845 William Lewis Gilbert bought Clarke's share in the company. Three years later, Clarke purchased his shares again. The partnership lasted until 1851. The company name became W. L. Gilbert & Company until 1866 when the Gilbert Manufacturing Company was established. Only 30 years following its purchase in 1871, the Winsted (or Winchester) factory burned down.

William L. Gilbert was not a quitter. He formed the William L. Gilbert Clock Company that very same year (1871). William Lewis Gilbert died in 1890, but the company name was retained for 63 years.

George B. Owen managed the clock company from 1880 to around 1900. Despite financial problems from 1934 to 1957, the company remained active as the William L. Gilbert Clock Corporation.

During World War 11 (1941-1945) clock production was limited. The war effort required metal. The clock company was allowed to manufacture papier-mâché case alarm clocks rather than metal ones. These clocks enabled workers to get to their war related jobs on time.

After the General Computing Company took over the Gilbert Company, the name General-Gilbert Corporation was used.

By 1964, the company clock division was no longer profitable. Spartus Corporation of Louisville, Mississippi, and Chicago purchased the former Gilbert Company.

The E. Ingraham Company

Elias Ingraham (1805-1885) founded the E. Ingraham Company. He served a five-year apprenticeship with Daniel Dewey as a cabinetmaker. In 1828 he went to work for George Mitchell, a wise businessman in Bristol, Connecticut. Mitchell wanted a worker who was creative and could produce new case styles. By succeeding in this task, Ingraham earned the reputation of being an innovative man in the clock industry. The exotic case he designed had mahogany columns, paw feet, turned rosettes, and carved baskets of fruit.

In 1830 Ingraham went to work for Chauncey and Lawson C. Ives to design cases for their clocks. One of his cases, which could accommodate a long drop of weights, was a triple-decker. In the three years that followed, he made almost 6,000 cases for the firm of Chauncey and Lawson C. Ives.

During the next ten years, Ingraham was involved in making clock cases, chairs and mirrors. He helped design a Gothic case, named a steeple clock, which became extremely popular. These smaller clocks rapidly replaced the large Empire-style cases.

In the mid 1840s, he formed a partnership with Brewster called Brewster and Ingraham. Members of the clock-making company were the Ingraham brothers, Elias and Andrew, and Elisha Brewster.

The Ingraham Company, with its various name changes and partners, was one of the world's largest clock makers. In 1855, the Ingraham factory in Bristol burned. The loss amounted to about $30,000. A new firm was formed when Elias Ingraham made his son Edward a partner in 1857. The business name, E. Ingraham & Company, was used from 1861 to 1880. In 1881, the name was changed to The E. Ingraham & Company. This name stayed as such until 1884 when it became The E. Ingraham Company. During this period, the company manufactured clocks with black-painted or japanned cases. Over 200 different models were built.

Some of its later products, from 1914 to 1942, were non-jeweled pocket watches, wrist watches, eight-day lever movement clocks, electric clocks, and pendulum clocks.

Clock making activities stopped at Bristol in 1967 when the company was sold to McGraw-Edison.

The following advertisement is taken word for word from a Brewster & Ingraham promotional public notice.

BREWSTER & INGRAHAMS
Have constantly on hand, at their FACTORY, in
Bristol, Conn.,
Their various Styles of Patent Spring Eight Day and Thirty Hour
Brass Clocks,
In Mahogany, Zebra, Rosewood and Black-Walnut Cases.
Also Gallery, Hall and Counting-House Eight Day Time-
Pieces of 10
Inches to 22 Inches in diameter, in Gilt, Mahogany and Black
Walnut Cases.
ALSO AN IMPROVED KIND OF EIGHT DAY AND
THIRTY HOUR MARINE TIME-PIECES,
All which are made in the best manner.
•••••••
The Proprietors are constantly present to attend to all orders,
whether large or small, at as low prices, regard being had to
quality, as at any other Factory in the country.
THEY HAVE ALSO A HOUSE AT
NO. 13 WALBROOK, CITY LONDON,
ENGLAND.
Where they keep constantly on hand a large assortment of the
above kinds of
Clocks, together with Eight Day and Thirty Hour
OG WEIGHT CLOCKS.
Please call and examine before purchasing elsewhere.
E. C. Brewster. E. Ingraham. A. Ingraham.

The New Haven Clock Company

With a capital of $20,000, the New Haven Clock Company was incorporated in the early 1850s. The president of the company was Hiram Camp who retained that title for 40 years.

The company was formed to produce inexpensive brass movements for the Jerome Manufacturing Company. The Jerome Company went bankrupt and had to sell its assets, including its manufacturing plant.

Good fortune arose when the New Haven Clock Company purchased the defunct Jerome Company. From that day in the mid 1850s, until the 1880s, the company experienced successful years. In addition to expanding its operations by making complete clocks, it promoted pocket watches and wrist watches. New Haven sales offices were located around the world in such cities as Liverpool, England, and Yokohama, Japan. Through catalogs, New Haven sold its own clocks, as well as those made by F. Kroeber of New York, E. Howard Company of Boston, and E. Ingraham & Company of Bristol. New Haven soon became one of the largest clock companies in the United States. Among the clocks produced were French clocks, jewelers' regulators, ebony and mahogany cabinet clocks, wall clocks, including calendar varieties, figure clocks (now called statue clocks), and tall-case hall clocks. This sales procedure, however, was discontinued in 1885. Only a small number of imported clocks were offered for sale. Clocks manufactured by other domestic clock companies were no longer marketed by New Haven Clock Company.

A novelty, the Flying Pendulum clock, was patented in the early 1880s. The New Haven Clock Company took control of the patent and improved its mechanism and design until it became one of the funniest and most attractive clocks ever produced. Its movement is unique. A flying ball takes the place of the pendulum. It was advertised as the best show-window attraction ever made, but it was not noted for its time keeping accuracy. This unique clock has been reproduced from time to time, and as recently as the late 1950s.

In 1910, the company offered a vast variety of clocks. From 1917-1956 the clock maker was a major producer of inexpensive watches. A corporation, The New Haven Clock and Watch Company, took over the company in 1946. Financial woes plagued New Haven from 1956-1959.

After 107 years in business, the New Haven Clock Company's facilities and products were sold at a public auction in March of 1960. One reason for the company's demise was a tremendous overproduction of its products that made it impossible to realize a profit.

Seth Thomas

Seth Thomas (1786-1859) became an apprentice in the cabinetmaker-joiner trade in the early 1800s. He worked with Silas Hoadley around 1808-1810, under the supervision of Eli Terry in the area near Waterbury, Connecticut. Eli Terry needed help to fulfill a contract for 4,000 hang-up wooden clocks, their movements, pendulums, dials, and hands. Thomas, as a joiner, assembled the clocks using his woodworking techniques. All clocks were in running order when he finished.

In 1810 Seth Thomas and Silas Hoadley bought Eli Terry's plant. They made tall-case clocks and 30-hour clocks with wooden movements. In 1813 Seth Thomas sold his share of the business to Silas Hoadley and bought a shop in Plymouth Hollow, Connecticut, where he made tall-case clocks with wooden movements. This shop would remain his work place until 1853.

In 1839, Seth Thomas changed from using wooden to 30-hour brass clock movements. Around 1850 he began to use springs instead of weights for clock power.

Thomas, who was primarily known for his clock affiliation, was also a good businessman. He diversified his financial interests and acquired a considerable amount of farmland. In the early 1800s at the age 48, he bought a cotton factory which he operated profitably until the Civil War began in 1861. By 1844, he had discontinued making wooden clocks. As a traditionalist he was reluctant to change his clock making methods, but the change to brass clock production was more profitable. Thomas' company was soon producing 20,000 brass clocks annually. At the height of his brass clock production he built a brass rolling mill called the Thomas Manufacturing Company.

From 1853 to 1865 the Seth Thomas Clock Company operated in Plymouth Hollow. After Thomas' death in 1859, his three sons—Aaron, Edward, and Seth Junior—carried on the business. Many new models of spring driven clocks were produced. Calendar clocks became an important part of their clock line.

The residents of Plymouth Hollow respected Seth Thomas for the industries he established in the town. To show their appreciation, the town was renamed Thomaston in his honor six years after his death.

In the 1880s, the Seth Thomas Clock Company employed about 825 people. Over 70 of these employees were children. The workers put in a ten-hour workday and were paid from $1.50 to $3.00 a day. Skilled mechanics were at the top of the pay scale while laborers were at the bottom. With this staff the company produced approximately $729,000 worth of clocks annually.

The Seth Thomas Company, in the hands of the family members, was a success. It holds the distinction of being the longest established American clock making company. Seth Thomas profited by his leadership ability. He was one of the wealthiest men in Connecticut at the time of his death in 1859.

In 1879, Seth Thomas Sons & Company and the Seth Thomas Clock Company were consolidated. In 1931 the Seth Thomas Clock Company, established in 1853, became a division of General Time Corporation. Seth Thomas' great grandson, Seth E. Thomas Jr., was chairman of the board until his death in 1932. The company's leadership passed out of the hands of the Thomas family and in 1970 became a division of Tally Industries.

Waterbury Clock Company

The Waterbury Clock Company was a major clock producer in the United States from 1857 to 1944, a period of almost ninety years. It was originally started as a branch of the Benedict & Burnham Manufacturing Company, the largest brass producer in Waterbury. The company manufactured rolled and drawn brass, copper, cabinet hardware. and lamp burners.

The Waterbury Company was originally located in the Benedict & Burnham shops until they found larger quarters in Waterbury, Connecticut. Its growth was so rapid that by 1873 a large plant was built and expanded several times. By the late 1800s Waterbury employed about 3,000 people and made over 20,000 watches and clocks daily.

Waterbury became internationally known in the 1870s when it had offices in Toronto, Canada, and Glasgow, Scotland.

Waterbury made and sold movements as well as complete clocks. By the turn of the century it had a business relationship with Sears Roebuck, one of the big mail-order houses. Many styles of Waterbury clocks were sold, including eight-day time and strike in oak cases, which sold for two dollars each.

In 1913, a Waterbury factory catalog illustrated over 400 styles of clocks, starting at $1.20 each. Included were alarm, carriage, French mantel, and tall-clocks. In the early 1890s they manufactured non-jeweled watches, including the famous dollar watch made for R. H. Ingersoll & Bros., and acted as selling agents for the Ithaca Calendar Clock Company. This latter affiliation lasted until 1891 when Waterbury introduced its own line of perpetual calendar clocks.

During the Depression of the 1930s the company went into receivership, and its case shop and clock making materials and parts were sold at auction. Waterbury's life as a clock and watch manufacturer ended when United States Time Corporation bought the company in 1944.

E. N. Welch Manufacturing Co.

Prior to 1831, Elisha Niles Welch (1809-1887) was in business with his father, George, who operated an iron foundry business in Bristol. They made weights and bells for clocks. When Elisha Welch formed a partnership with Thomas Barnes Junior, the company was called Barnes & Welch. They manufactured wooden movement shelf clocks. Barnes and Welch were involved in business with Jonathan C. Brown and Chauncey Pomeroy.

From 1841-1849, E. N. Welch became a partner of J. C. Brown who used Forestville Manufacturing Company and J. C. Brown, Bristol, Connecticut, as company names. Chauncey Pomeroy was also a partner in these companies. Manufactured in these two factories were eight-day clocks with brass movements. In 1853 fire destroyed J. C. Brown's Forestville Hardware and Clock Company.

Welch bought Elisha Manross' failing clock parts business and J. C. Brown's Forestville Company after it went bankrupt. He also purchased the case making business of Frederick S. Otis. He consolidated these purchases under one name, E. N. Welch, which became one of Bristol's largest clock companies.

In 1868, the Welch, Spring and Company was formed. Their production emphasis was on high-quality clocks, including regulators and calendars. After Elisha Welch's death in 1887, his son James became the company's president. Fire destroyed the movement factory in 1899. Later that same year, the case factory met the same fate.

Financial problems plagued the company. Mortgages were past due. Bank notes were due and unpaid. Liabilities were growing and legal suits were pending. The company had no funds. Realizing the troubles that faced the Welch Clock makers, the Sessions family, who had a clock business in Forestville and were interested in expanding their business, began buying Welch company stock. After Albert L. Sessions became treasurer and W. E. Sessions assumed the presidency, they borrowed over $50,000 to revitalize the company.

At this time the Welch Company ceased to exist, and the name was changed to the Sessions Clock Company.

The Welch, Spring, & Company

The Welch, Spring & Company was organized by three clock enthusiasts—Elisha Niles Welch, Solomon Crosby Spring, and Benjamin Bennet Lewis. Their partnership lasted for 16 years, from 1868-1884.

Each of these men brought a talent which contributed to the success of the organization. Welch was the financier, Spring was the manager and design engineer, and Lewis was the inventor. These men were interested in developing a superior, quality clock line. This was contrary to the operational techniques of the major clock companies in America where their success was based on quantity rather than quality.

At the age of 22 Welch formed a partnership with Thomas Barnes using a Barnes and Welch label as their company's logo. On two separate occasions, in 1841 and again in 1880, he loaned money to J. C. Brown, a fellow clock maker. When Brown's company became insolvent, Welch purchased it from him as well as two other Bristol firms—The Forestville Hardware and Clock Company and The Frederick Otis Case Shop. He consolidated these clock holdings under the name of E. N. Welch Manufacturing Company. Since he was a wise and cautious investor, his projects always seemed to be successful. It was largely due to Welch's support that the Welch, Spring & Co. succeeded.

Lewis' contribution to the new company was his ability to develop calendar mechanisms. Three patents for perpetual calendar mechanisms were issued to him on Feb. 4, 1862, June 21, 1864, and Dec. 29, 1868.

The last member of this new company, Spring, was a renowned case-maker who specialized in rosewood cases. He learned basic techniques while working for the Atkins Clock Company. After leaving this company, he spent about 20 years operating his own business. Following the purchase of the defunct Birge, Peck, and Company, he named it S. C. Spring Clock Company. This newly organized company supplied cases, movements, and parts to clock makers in the Bristol, Connecticut, area. He also manufactured vast numbers of clocks for the parent company.

The Welch, Spring & Company passed through four stages during its sixteen operational years. The first stage, from 1868-1869, marked the period that was devoted to creating a standard shelf model. Three models—the Empress, the Peerless, and the Italian—were produced.

During the second stage, lasting from 1870-1876, emphasis was on the production of regulators and calendar clocks. Only five styles of regulators and five styles of calendars were made. All of the calendar clocks used the B. B. Lewis perpetual calendar mechanism. Case options were walnut or rosewood.

Although the majority of their No. 1 regulators were made with rosewood cases, the walnut case model became rare and expensive due to the small number that were made. Originally they sold for $95, a price too high for the average American buyer. In the other four regulator models, walnut and rosewood were the wood choices.

The third stage, from 1877-1888, concentrated on selecting names for the clocks which stood for quality and which the public knew. At this time, other manufacturers used names of cities, regents, and rivers for their clock series. A decision was made by Spring and the staff members to use the names of popular artists from the opera and theater as clock names. The Spring models of 1877 included seven artists—Parepa, Lucca, Titiens, Verdi, Kellogg, Auber, and Wagner. These selections were composers and opera singers.

The variety of clock styles on which these names were to be used included shelf clocks, regulators, wall octagons, and shelf and wall calendar clocks. The two shelf clocks in rosewood were the Parepa and the Lucca. The latter was also made as a regulator and the Titiens, a shelf clock, had a walnut case. The octagon wall clock was the Verdi, and the wall regulator in walnut was the Kellogg. The other two, the Auber, a shelf calendar clock, and the Wagner, in both a wall and shelf calendar, had black walnut cases.

The fourth and final stage, called the Patti Era, lasted for five years from 1879-1884. This developmental period was named for Adelina Patti (1843-1919), a Spanish coloratura soprano who won fame as one of the world's greatest operatic singers. Her career was almost without parallel in the history of the operatic stage.

This period marked the company's final effort to be financially successful. The staff felt that the company's success would depend on the success of the Patti model. The original Patti clock was known for its fancy column turnings, glass sides, rosettes, and fancy finials. Its case was rosewood and it had a Sandwich glass pendulum. The Patti was considered by many as the most collectible and famous parlor clock ever conceived by an American manufacturer. However, sales did not live up to expectations.

The company tried to dress up the Patti to improve its sales. A brass pendulum with a Sandwich glass center and a gold leaf border on the glass door panel were added. Black labels with gold print replaced the white labels with black print. A bell mounted on the movement and French-style cloverleaf hands were added.

These changes, however, did not solve the company's problem. The demise of Welch, Spring, & Company came as a result of the expense required to produce these ornate clocks that were too expensive for the public to buy.

In 1884, the company ceased doing business. All of the buildings, inventory and machinery of the Welch, Spring & Company was purchased by E. N. Welch for $10,000. The mass production concept had won, and the ornate "Patti" clocks failed to appeal to the average citizen because of their high cost.

Despite this, E. N. Welch died a wealthy man in 1887, leaving an estate of approximately three million dollars.

Ansonia "Senator" oak statue shelf clock with brass and silver-plated decorations, circa 1880; eight-day, time and strike, spring driven, 15" wide, 10" deep, 22" high, 6" dial; $1,600.

Ansonia Brass & Copper Company rosewood round top, short-drop wall clock, circa 1854-59, eight-day, time and strike, spring driven, 24" high, 11" dial; $400.

W. L. Gilbert walnut round top, short-drop simple calendar clock with G. Maranville's calendar movement, patent 1861, eight-day, time only, spring driven, 17-1/2" wide, 33-1/2" high, 14-1/2" dial; $1,500.

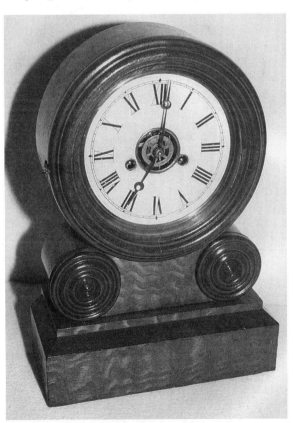

E. Ingraham "Grecian" zebrawood veneered shelf clock, circa 1880, 30-hour, time and strike, spring driven, 10" wide, 14-1/2" high, 6" dial; $325.

New Haven oak wall regulator, early 1900s, eight-day, time and strike, spring driven, 16" wide, 35" high; $425.

New Haven "Number 2" oak round top, long-drop regulator, circa 1900, 30-day, time and strike, 35" high, 11-1/2" dial; $700.

Seth Thomas miniature OG mahogany veneered shelf clock with S and T on hands for Seth Thomas, after 1865, 30-hour, time, strike, and alarm, 10" wide, 16" high; $150.

Seth Thomas mahogany wall clock, circa 1900, 30-day, time and strike, spring driven, 19-1/2" wide, 30" high, 7" dial; $550.

Waterbury walnut, double-dial perpetual calendar shelf clock, A. F. Well's, July 30, 1889, patent calendar movement, eight-day, time and strike, spring driven, 16-1/2" wide, 29" high, 7" dials; $1,400.

E.N. Welch walnut shelf clocks. Left: eight-day, time and strike, spring driven, 17" wide, 28-1/2" high, 5" dial; $700. Right: eight-day, time and strike, spring driven, 14" wide, 28" high, 5" dial; $700.

Welch, Spring, & Company rosewood wall clock, circa 1868-84, eight-day, time and strike, weight driven, 15" wide, 40" high; $8,000-$9,000.

Chapter 5

Histories of Other Clock Makers

E. Howard Clock Company

Edward Howard (1813-1904) was a clock maker in the early 1800s when he served an apprenticeship under the supervision of Aaron Willard Jr. With him as an apprentice was David P. Davis.

After the completion of their apprenticeships, Howard and Davis formed a partnership that also included Luther Stephenson. They were located in Boston under the firm name of Stephenson, Howard & Davis and practiced their trade until the mid 1840s. Despite the exodus of Stephenson from the company, business was carried on until the late 1850s. At this time, Davis also quit, leaving Howard alone in the reorganized E. Howard & Co. situated in Roxbury, Massachusetts.

Howard made banjo, regulator, and turret clocks. Howard's reputation as a manufacturer of high quality clocks with high prices has kept his clocks in the "highly sought after" category. Some of his astronomical regulators are priced in the $15,000 plus range. Singularly rare and costly are the sidewalk or post clocks which are probably all in the hands of private collectors and as such are almost never seen at public auctions or sales.

If you find a Howard Clock and purchase it, keep it as is, rather than refinishing it. The clock will lose value if its finish is changed.

In 1958, clock production stopped with the exception of tower clocks, which were made until 1964.

Ithaca Calendar Clock Company

The Ithaca Calendar Clock Company was established in 1865 using Henry B. Horton's perpetual roller-type calendar clock patent. Two calendar clock patents were issued to him, one on April 18, 1865, and the other on August 28, 1866, which was an improvement on his first patent. Because Horton's clock was a perpetual calendar clock, it could be adjusted automatically to accommodate Leap Year.

The Ithaca Calendar Clock Company specialized in only making calendar clocks. Henry Bishop Horton (1819-1885) could not find men in the Connecticut area to use his mechanism in their clocks. He was independent enough, however, to establish a factory in Ithaca, New York where the cases and calendar mechanisms were made.

From about 1855 until the turn of the century, calendar clocks were very popular and the larger companies manufactured several models of them. On most of the calendar clocks, corrections were made for the irregular number of days in different months and for leap year because a simple calendar device was used. By using a perpetual calendar system, no manual changes would have to be made for the entire year.

The clock faces on the Ithaca clocks were made up of two circular dials, one above the other. The time was indicated on the top dial while the bottom dial showed the date of the month, the day of the week and the month of the year. In most cases the two dials have the same diameter, but in some cases the top dial is smaller than the bottom one.

These unique clocks were shipped to various parts of the world and were available in 15 different languages. Calendar clocks were produced in great numbers after 1850. Most ran for eight days, although some 30-day clocks existed. Painted cases, as well as those made from walnut or rosewood, were available.

Unfortunately, in 1876 a fire destroyed the Ithaca clock factory. Destructive fires were common occurrences among clock companies. Undaunted, Henry Horton secured another building and business continued as usual.

The business began to decline after 1900 and finally went bankrupt. Perpetual calendar clocks are extremely expensive to buy today. Prices can soar to heights of $4,000 and more.

The direction label that follows was found on the outside of the back of an Ithaca Calendar clock. We print it here to show you how exacting a company can be about its product. Also the public is informed in the last sentence, "No women or children are employed in these works."

Ithaca Calendar Clock Co.
Ithaca, N. Y.
DIRECTIONS
The pendulum Ball and Key will be found fastened either at the bottom or top of the clock
The time now stands at 5 minutes before 11 P.M.
If the clock is to be set IN THE MORNING, turn the minute hand forward until the right hour is reached.
If the clock is to be set IN THE AFTERNOON, turn the minute hand forward through TWELVE HOURS and then to the right hour.
The calendar changes at midnight.
Set the clock in position and attach the pendulum ball.
The clock must be perpendicular to insure a perfect beat.
NEVER MOVE THE HOUR HAND by itself, as the calendar would not change at the proper hour.
TO SET THE CALENDAR - Raise the wire on the top of the clock and turn the calendar hand forward (never backward) until the right
month and day of month is shown.
Still holding up the wire turn the day of the week UPWARD till right.
CAUTION — USE NO OIL ON THE CALENDAR. It is not needed, and

will work only injury when used by attracting dust and clogging the machine.

TO REGULATE THE TIME — Raise or lower the pendulum all by means of the nut below it.

If the clock does not strike correctly, raise the small wire at the left under the seat on which rests the time movement, and repeat until it strikes correctly. But this cannot be done within 15 minutes of the striking hour. This clock strikes the half hours.

THE BEST TIME TO CORRECT THE STRIKE IS IMMEDIATELY AFTER THE HOUR IS STRUCK.

This Clock is set for 19___

Every clock before leaving the works is tested thoroughly, both as to time and Calendar, and the Calendar being set on the right year when the clock is packed, will give the Leap year and other Februarys correctly unless interfered with, or worked ahead of time. But if this should occur, it can readily be set right as follows: Raise the wire as above, turn the pointer forward until a February is shown, and then place the pointer on the Figure 29, drop the wire and if the pointer cannot be moved you have a Leap Year February. If the pointer is not hold fast on the figure 29, continue the process until it is. Calling this the Last Leap Year, work forward as before to the right year and month.

No women or children are employed in these works.

Joseph Ives

Joseph Ives (1782-1862) of Connecticut was both an inventor and a clock maker. Wooden clock movements were in vogue when Joseph entered the clock trade. He followed this trend and fashioned wooden movements. Soon, however, he felt that brass ones would be better, especially those made from rolled sheet brass. He developed a rolling pinion, a small gear with teeth that fit into those of a larger gear or rack. Normally it has fewer than 20 teeth that are referred to as leaves.

In addition, Joseph Ives received a patent for a steel spring. He is credited with a possible American first when he developed this successful clock spring. Up until this time, only English clock makers made and used steel springs successfully.

He headed the Joseph Ives & Co. of Bristol, Connecticut from 1818-1819. Sometime later, Joseph Ives was credited with being the inventor of the wagon spring clock. He used these flat springs to power clock movements. Around 1826, Joseph moved to Brooklyn, New York, and for a period of about five years made wagon spring clocks. He served as a guiding light for the Ives business interests until his death in 1862.

Among his clock creations are the "Duncan Phyfe" or "Brooklyn" type wagon spring clock. The dial on this clock is decorated with a vase of flowers and a picture is painted on the tablet. He also developed a wagon spring one-month clock, which winds at the 2 and 10 numbers rather than the 4 and 8 where most clocks wind. This clock is time only. Other Ives clocks include a 30-day wagon spring in a drop octagon; a "Connecticut Lyre" eight-day wall clock with a gold leaf front decoration, and the hour glass one-day wagon spring clock with a label that reads: "Plainville, Conn.".

It is possible that the Ives brothers inherited their interest in clocks from their father, Amas Ives of Bristol, who worked from 1770-1790.

There were six Ives brothers—Ira (1775-1848), Amasa (1777-1817), Philo (1780-1822), Joseph (1782-1862), Shaylor (1785-1840), and Chauncey (1787-1857).

One author said that these brothers gained fame when they became an integral part of Bristol clock history. Amazingly this group of brothers had a total of eleven patents on clocks. Ira received two, one for a time and strike clock and another for pinions. Shaylor had two for clock springs, and Joseph earned seven patents. All these men were a credit to their profession and each one of them produced quality clocks.

F. Kroeber Clock Company

The name F. Kroeber Clock Company conjures up pictures of costly clocks. They are rarely available to the moderate buyer. The maker of these clocks was Florence Kroeber (1840-1911) who was born in Germany in 1840. He and his family crossed the Atlantic Ocean in the mid-1800s and settled in New York City.

At the age of 19, Kroeber was employed as a bookkeeper in the Owen and Clark Clock Store. George B. Owen operated the business when Clark left the company in 1861. Soon, George B. Owen left to become general manager of the W. L. Gilbert Clock Company in Winsted, Connecticut. This gave Florence Kroeber the opportunity to acquire the business. Clocks made in the United States as well as imported ones were featured in his store. European novelties were also stocked.

When a German immigrant sought employment in 1868, F. Kroeber accepted this man, Nicholas Mueller, as a partner, who specialized in producing bronzed cast metal figurines and inscribed metal clock case fronts. This relationship only lasted about a year.

Advertisements during the beginning of the 1870s listed Kroeber as an "Importer and dealer in French, German and American clocks."

Florence Kroeber began to create clock cases. He ordered movements from Connecticut makers. His clock business was successful, and it was incorporated as the F. Kroeber Clock Company. A second store was opened in Manhattan's midtown area. In order to stock his store with interesting novelties, he traveled to Europe in the spring of 1888 where he bought a miscellany of novelties—wood cased pieces, nickel and brass items, vases, candelabra, bronze figures and plush covered novelties.

Until 1899, Kroeber created clock cases. A couple of them, patented in 1869 looked like Victorian picture frames. Kroeber sometimes used metal cases that came from other companies.

Both marble and china cases were imported and received American movements. Kroeber, at times, coated cast-iron clock cases so that they resembled porcelain. He called his patented product, "Porcelene." Soon Ansonia Clock Company produced clocks with the same porcelain-type finish and colors. Kroeber sued Ansonia for infringing on his patent. Kroeber also patented a pendulum that did not have to be taken off when a clock was moved.

F. Kroeber's 1888 catalog displayed more than 250 clocks of which over 90% of the stock was of American manufacture. However, business was poor as a result of the Depression of 1893 and Kroeber was forced to close one store and move into smaller quarters. Unfortunately he went bankrupt in January 1904.

He no longer owned a clock company, and for seven years worked as a clerk in a store watch and clock department. Florence Kroeber died on May 16, 1911 from tuberculosis.

Today, examples of his quality clocks today are appreciated by people who enjoy collecting unique, hard to find clocks. Collectors realize that his clocks bring higher prices and are more difficult to find than those made by some of the major clock companies.

It is suspected, but not proved, that Kroeber put his label on some mass-produced American and imported clocks. Kroeber did have a known label that stated, "F. Kroeber, agent for New Haven, E. N. Welch, Jerome, Seth Thomas and other companies".

Collectors should carefully inspect a clock that is reputed to be a Kroeber product. A Kroeber label, dial, or marked Kroeber movement make the clock desirable as well as costly, but it must be determined that there are no reproduction parts. A specialist in Kroeber clocks can be of great assistance.

As an aid in dating Kroeber clocks, the information that follows may answer questions relating to the age of a specific clock.

City Directory Research: Kroeber

Name of Company	Address	Date
F. Kroeber	25 John St.	1865 – 1869
	10 Cortlandt St.	1869 – 1874
	8 Cortlandt St.	1874 – 1882
	14 Cortlandt St.	1883 – Feb. 1887
F. Kroeber Clock Company	14 Cortlandt St.	Feb. 1887 – Dec. 1887
	360 Broadway	Jan. 1888 – 1892
	360 Broadway & 14 Union Square*	1892 – March 1895
	360 Broadway	March 1895 – May 1899
F. Kroeber & Company	14 Maiden Lane	May 1899 – Feb. 1904
Mueller & Kroeber	25 John St. or 66 Beekman St.	1868 – 1869

*Clocks may not have been labeled with both addresses, so 360 Broadway may have been used January 1888 through May 1899.

Lux and Keebler

Before establishing the Lux Clock Company in 1917, Paul Lux worked for the Waterbury Clock Company. His family, including his wife and two sons, Fred and Herman, worked together for several years trying to form a clock company that would make novelty clocks. Despite a fire that delayed their project and their sons marching off to fight in World War I,

their perseverance and help from friends moved the project forward. Their motto "Our clocks Must Go–or We Go" became a motivational factor. When the two boys returned home from service, Lux clocks were ready to market.

Another company associated with Lux was the Keebler Company in Chicago. Its founder, August C. Keebler, had Lux make clocks for him. A reciprocal agreement stated that each company could sell the same clocks, but they must be marketed with different names. Consequently, the Lux and Keebler pendulettes resulted.

A compressed molded wood was used in the manufacture of these clocks. In pendulette versions, a black cat could swing his pendulum tail as his eyes moved. Castles, bull dogs, clowns, Rudolf the Red Nose Reindeer, Woody Woodpecker, flowers, a pirate, the Empire State Building, plus many more objects or animals were themes on these pendulettes. Many of these clocks are illustrated in Chapter 10: Novelty Clocks.

Clocks other than pendulettes featured current events, people, comic characters, patriotic themes, the Boy Scouts, and people ranging from Sally Rand (the fan dancer) to President Franklin D. Roosevelt.

The Lux variety of novelty clocks is seemingly endless. These fun clocks cause people to smile. Owners of some examples can smile too when they think of how their values have soared. The price range for these Lux wall clocks starts at $250 and climbs to a phenomenal price of $3,500. The latter price is for the "Christmas Wreath".

Eli Terry

In 1792-1793 Eli Terry, Sr. showed that he was a man with creative ideas. He asked, "Why make one clock only?" It was easier to complete parts for several clocks at the same time, and Terry proceeded to do so. The floor standing clocks he made were originally called long case or tall case clocks. Now they are referred to as grandfather clocks. Shorter versions are called grandmother clocks.

From 1806-1809, Terry made 4,000 hang-up clock movements, dials, hands, and pendulums. He invented machines that assisted him with his work, including one that cut gear wheel teeth. His employees, Silas Hoadley and Seth Thomas, assisted him. The environs of Waterbury, Connecticut provided the waterpower. In 1810 Silas Hoadley and Seth Thomas bought Terry's plant. Eli moved to Plymouth Hollow, Connecticut where he continued his work.

It was in about 1816 that Terry patented a shelf clock that had a new outside escapement movement in the pillar and scroll case. Soon, around 1818-1824, the three Terry men, Eli Sr., Eli Jr., and Henry organized the firm Eli Terry and Sons of Plymouth, Connecticut. Their pillar and scroll clock sold well. Each had a label that proclaimed: "Patent clock invented by Eli Terry made and sold at Plymouth, Connecticut by Eli Terry and Sons." The eight-day triple-decker clock was 34 to 38 inches high.

Terry clock labels varied and dates on them frequently overlapped. Here are examples: 1824-1827 Eli and brother Samuel were listed on the labels; 1824-1830 an Eli Terry Jr. label appeared; from 1825-1830 Eli Terry and son Henry were located in Plymouth according to the label; from 1830-1841 Eli Terry Jr. and Company was also listed at Plymouth.

On December 22, 1831, Eli Terry the well-known clock creator was honored when the town name became Terrysville. In about 1834, Eli Terry Sr. retired after a financially profitable career. However, in order to keep busy he made brass movement clocks during his retirement years.

In the late 1840s, Silas Burnham Terry, Eli's youngest son, established the S. B. Terry Company to make clocks.

Eli Terry, the noted clock maker, died in 1852 in the town that changed its name to honor him. His descendants did not forget their heritage. In 1852 Silas Burnham Terry and his son founded the Terry Clock Company in Winsted, Connecticut. Son Silas was its president. The company remained in business until 1876. It is interesting that the spelling of the town name was changed slightly in 1872. By deleting the "s" Terrysville became Terryville.

The Willard Brothers

Four of the Willard brothers were clock makers. Their names were: Benjamin (1743-1803), the third child of 12 siblings, Simon (1753-1848), the eighth born, Ephram (life line not available), the ninth born, and Aaron (1757-1844), the tenth child. Very little has been written about Ephram and his activities. He apparently worked for a while in the area where his siblings worked, including Roxbury, Massachusetts. In 1798, he left to reside elsewhere. He is listed as a New York resident in 1805.

After completing his apprenticeship in 1764, Benjamin began making clocks in Grafton, Massachusetts. He soon moved to Boston and he opened a shop on Roxbury Street where a colony of artists resided. There he made a variety of clock styles. In 1773 he ran an advertisement in the Boston Gazette that read: "Benjamin Willard at his shop in Roxbury Street ... has on sale musical clocks playing different tunes every day of the week and on Sunday a psalm tune." He further stated: "The music plays once every hour and does not obstruct the clock's motion in any way."

Simon was the second brother to enter the clock making trade. He became the most famous of the four siblings. Tall case clocks (called grandfathers now) were the norm until Simon helped introduce shelf and wall clocks. Around 1800, he began working on an eight-day wall clock. It was patented on February 8, 1892, as his "Improved Timepiece." The pendulum was suspended from the front with the weight at the bottom that allowed the pendulum to be screwed down. This meant that the clock could be moved without damaging the suspension. Because of its shape, it was called a banjo clock. The first ones were time only. There was a clear seven-inch dial, fine hands and a mahogany case. The glass was decorated with gold leaf. The weight driven movement was so accurate that, "it kept well within one minute's error a week." This beautiful instrument won acclaim at once and is still a popular style. Naturally others desired to create similar clocks. They had to make slight changes, however, so as not to infringe on Simon's patent. Simon advertised that he made clocks for church steeples as well as eight-day timepieces. In a 38-year time-span, this man made approximately 4,000 clocks.

A Simon Willard 92-inch high grandfather clock with a white iron dial plus moon and calendar configuration is on display at the Henry Ford Museum.

The Lighthouse clock was invented by Simon Willard of Roxbury, Massachusetts, who patented it in 1822. It has an octagonal base, a mahogany case, tapered circular trunk and a glass dome covering the eight-day alarm movement. An engraved brass dial with arrow hands finishes off this clock. The clock may be seen at the Metropolitan Museum of Art.

Aaron Willard made banjo clocks, and with his brothers' help created 30-hour wall timepieces. Soon, they and other makers fashioned the earliest known American shelf clocks. Their cases looked like the top section of tall case clocks and they earned the name "The Massachusetts Half Clocks."

The Willard Brothers contributed ideas that promoted and expanded the clock industry. Their clocks, with their precise workmanship, were durable and ran well due in part to the use of hard brass in their manufacture.

E. Howard & Company "Model 75" walnut wall clock, circa 1875-80; eight-day, time only, weight driven, 9-3/4" wide at base, 15-1/4 " wide at top, 33" high, 11-1/2" dial; $3,000.

Ithaca "Cottage" walnut Calendar Clock with double dial, H. B. Horton's Calendar patents, April 18, 1865, and August 28, 1866; eight-day, time and strike, spring driven 12" wide, 25" high, 5" upper dial, 7" lower dial; $1,000.

F. Kroeber wall clocks. Left: "Scythia" ebony finished wall clock with beveled mirror at base, circa 1884, eight-day, time and strike, spring driven, 9-3/4" wide, 27" high, porcelain dial; $1,500. Right: "Reflector" ebony finished wall clock with mirrors at sides, a drawer at base, open escapement and porcelain dial, patented date March 7, 1884 on pendulum, eight-day, time and strike, spring driven, 13" wide, 32" high; $1,500.

Lux molded wood pendulette wall clocks with cuckoo clocks at each end, 30-hour, time only, spring driven, 6" wide, 13" to 15" high; $125 each.

Eli Terry pendulum candlestick novelty clock with china base on wooden frame, 6" diameter, 9" high, time only, original glass dome missing; $300.

Chapter 6
Old Timers

It was a status symbol in the 1700s to own a clock. Clocks were handcrafted, and were made only when an affluent person placed an order. The clock maker frequently melted down the brass in his own furnace, cast it, hammered it, turned it, and filed it. The dial, the hands, the works, the case—the total clock—were completed in the same shop. Apprentices assisted as they learned the trade. Very few people could afford to buy a clock so painstakingly constructed.

The following eight artisans, applying their particular skills, were employed in making patent clocks: 1) the carpenter who made the cases, 2) the foundry man who formed the finials, 3) the artist who painted the glass tablet, 4) the goldsmith who made the gold leaf, 5) the die-maker who made the hands, 6) the craftsman who imported and applied the veneers to the cases, 7) the glue-makers who secured the dowels and blocks to keep the case together, and 8) the wood carver and the stencil artisan who added embellishments.

A public or town clock was mentioned in town records as early as 1650. It was felt by the townspeople throughout the colonies that every town needed a town clock.

Because handcrafted clocks required so many processes, a learner or apprentice needed the supervision of a master craftsman. A youth began his training at about fourteen years of age and was bound by contract to a tradesman for seven years. The master taught the youth all aspects of the trade from the simple to the complex until he became efficient. He was paid no wages, but did receive room and board in his tutor's home. Because of the free labor provision, the clock maker's business often increased and provided him with additional revenue. At the completion of his apprenticeship, the worker was given a letter of recommendation from his master. An example of such a letter dated July 13, 1796, follows:

> This is to certify that Daniel Monroe, Jun. had served an apprenticeship of seven years with me the Subscriber, that he had been uncommonly faithful, honest, and industrious, and that I hereby acknowledge him capable of making any work that I manufacture and that I do pronounce him as one of the best workmen in America (signed) Simon Willard.

During the 1770s brass founders did the initial preparation of the metal. By 1780, however, cast brass parts could be purchased, and the clock makers did the turning, gear cutting, filing, and assembly. The industry was beginning to diversify, as different craftsmen became involved in the clock making process.

Extensive clock making was carried out in the colonies of Delaware, Maryland, Virginia, North Carolina, South Carolina, Georgia, Rhode Island, and New Hampshire. The clock making activities and the names of the men involved would provide the reader with a mini history of this colonial trade.

In the beginning of colonial clock making, the handcrafted methods limited both the quantity manufactured and the production of inexpensive clocks. When the use of waterpower to operate machinery was introduced, production increased to a great extent.

Around the middle of the 18th century, Philadelphia was thought of as the place where the repairing of clocks and watches, the building of cases, and the constructing of clock movements was centralized. The principal products of the Philadelphia area were tall clocks in addition to some bracket clocks. The bracket clock has been erroneously called a mantel clock, but because it stands on a matching bracket affixed to a wall, this name is incorrect. Also, bracket clocks predated mantel clocks by about 50 years. These bracket and tall clocks were not the result of mass production. The clock makers, as artisans, followed their tradition of handcrafting their products. This method of clock making decreased to such an extent that by 1850 few clocks were handcrafted in the Philadelphia area. Their inability to compete with the Connecticut clock makers, who produced inexpensive clocks, caused their eventual demise.

Perhaps the most noted clock maker from the Philadelphia school was David Rittenhouse, who was a mathematician, surveyor, astronomer and clock maker. His most outstanding creation was a nine-foot masterpiece that could play ten musical tunes on fifteen bells. This clock, made in 1774, originally sold for $640 and can be seen at the Drexel Institute in Philadelphia.

The Shakers, who established themselves in upstate New York after the Revolution, carried out some clock making. Their creations were usually without ornate decorations or striking mechanisms. The earliest Shaker clock maker was Amos Jewett (1753-1834) who made tall clocks with printed paper dials. He numbered his clocks so they could be easily identified. For example, number 12 was made in 1789 and number 38 was made seven years later.

The Boston area is known for the Willard Family who became prominent clock makers. Two of the sons, Benjamin and Ephraim, mainly produced tall clocks, while Simon and Aaron produced shelf clocks as well as tall clocks. Some clocks attributed to the brothers include a miniature shelf clock, circa 1780, by Aaron; a patent alarm Lighthouse Clock, circa 1833, by Simon; and a kidney dial shelf clock, circa 1795, by Aaron.

Simon Willard was proud of his newly invented Alarum Timepiece and touted it in an advertisement that read "...will run 8 days with once winding, and keep exact time; there is an alarum affixed to them, which, when set, will not fail to go off at the hour you wish to rise. The case is about 16 inches high, and easily moved to any part of the house without putting it out or order. The whole of the clock works is enclosed with a handsome glass, and is wound up without taking it off, which prevents the dirt from getting into it."

Wooden movements, which were easier to make and less costly than hand-fashioned brass movements, came into use around 1800. Cases for clocks were most often made of mahogany despite the fact that it was more expensive than the wood that was available locally. In Pennsylvania, for example, cases were made of walnut and maple and in New England pine and cherry were used.

Three unique shelf clocks are the cottage, beehive and acorn. The acorn clock, in both a shelf and wall style, is American in origin. The Forestville Manufacturing Co. made them all. Jonathan Clarke Brown was the manager of this company during the mid 1800s. Eight-day fusee movements were utilized in these clocks.

The cottage clock, first made around 1875, is a smaller form of the Connecticut shelf clock. Most examples have 30-hour movements and wooden cases that are normally less than one foot in height with tops that were either flat or three-sided. Most were made in the last quarter of the 19th century.

Paper dials in books of 24, 48, or 96 could be purchased in the late 1700s. These were pasted on wooden panels or iron plates to form clock faces.

Clock works, run by falling weights, required large cases to provide an adequate dropping space. For this reason, early weight driven shelf clocks were tall.

Clocks with heavy weights were expensive to ship. Because of this, empty "tin cans" (sheet-iron cans), instead of the heavy weights, were shipped with the clocks. The recipient then could fill these containers with sand or stones to achieve the weight necessary to operate the clock properly.

Simon Willard patented the banjo wall clock in 1802. He called it his "Improved Timepiece" but it was dubbed "banjo" because it resembled that instrument in shape. The "banjo" was a native American type and not a copy of a previously produced European clock. Originally it was time only, and reputedly cost $35.

The girandole clock, credited to Lemuel Curtis, is similar in design but larger than the banjo clock with a circular rather than a rectangular base frame. It has carved acanthus leaves as a decorative touch. Produced between 1814 and 1829, it is considered by many as the most beautiful clock case ever created in America. An ornately carved American eagle was frequently poised at the top of the clock.

Among the pictured banjo wall clocks found in this book are several expensive and hard to find examples by E. Howard & Company. Another rare banjo wall clock with its Westminster chimes is the Ansonia "Girandole."

The E. Howard Clock Company, led by Edward Howard (1813-1904), who had served as an apprentice to Aaron Willard at the age of 16, produced a series of banjo regulators as seen in an 1858 company catalog. He eventually became a prominent maker of clocks, including banjos, figure-eights, regulators, grandfathers, wall and tower clocks. The latter clocks were built into towers or steeples of public buildings for the public's use. Several of these models have been reproduced. Howard's clocks rank higher in value than most of the other manufactured clocks of like kind.

The long case clock, commonly called a grandfather clock, was first made in England in the latter part of the 17th century, shortly after the Restoration of 1660. Similar clocks were also appearing in Europe around this time. These clocks were approximately seven feet high with brass dials until painted ones appeared around 1770.

Until the introduction of mahogany, clock cases were walnut with marquetry designs. Satinwood and rosewood were two other woods used. Oak was used, too, but only for a cheaper clock. The cases for the movements hid the pendulum and weights and also kept it dust free. Often these cases were made of highly polished wood, adorned with rich ornamental touches. The dial was richly decorated and the mechanism contained bells of various sizes, which struck on the hours and quarter hours.

Later these clocks registered the month, date of the month and day of the week. At the end of the 17th century, a good London-made grandfather clock would cost in the proximity of $60 with a highly polished walnut and ebony case.

Called hall, tall, floor or long case, these were the first clocks to be made in the colonies. They were made throughout the colonies and were modifications of the English styles. Clock makers, in general, copied the styles and patterns used in their homeland.

All of the colonies were responsible for the manufacture of some long case clocks, but it was Pennsylvania and Massachusetts that produced the greatest number. These early clocks had either a brass or wooden movement and operated for one day or eight days.

A Simon Willard grandfather clock is on display at the Henry Ford Museum in Greenfield Village, Dearborn, Michigan. Also there on display is a typical Thomas Harland clock, 89-1/2 inches high, made around 1780. He was a renowned clock maker and the first to use interchangeable parts and mass production principles from 1791 onwards. Another one of Harland's grandfather clocks is on display at the Metropolitan Museum of Art in New York City.

At the Henry Francis du Pont Winterthur Museum, in Winterthur, Delaware, is a tall clock with a case of tulip poplar. It has a brass movement and was created by David Rittenhouse in 1755.

The Waltham Clock Company made reproductions of the Willard Banjo clocks as listed in their 1928 catalog. The cases were solid mahogany or walnut with gilt or crackle finishes. Each had the option of having a brass eagle or carved acorn as a top ornament. There were many choices of glass panel subjects as can be seen by the following: Washington–Mt. Vernon; Lone Ship; English Castle; Boston State House; Monticello–Jefferson; Perry's Victory; Wayside Inn; Independence Hall–Liberty Bell; Constitution and Guerriere; and Old Ironsides.

Among those clock makers who plied their trade before the advent of manufacturing was Thomas Harland of Norwich, Connecticut, who came to the American colonies from London in 1773. He worked for approximately 35 years, had many apprentices, and probably produced more tall clocks than any other Connecticut tradesman. His yearly production may have averaged about 25 clocks. Among his talents were making and repairing watches and clocks and also making musical and spring driven timepieces. Attributed to Harland is a musical bracket clock made in 1780 that was the envy of local tradesmen. One of his clocks played six tunes. Upon his death in 1807, he left an estate of $3,500 that was valued in tin wear, clocks, watches, jewelry and tradesman's tools

The American Empire Period, spanning the years 1825-1840, followed the Federal and preceded the Victorian period. Representative clocks of this period include the looking glass and the triple-decker. These eight-day, mahogany veneered clocks were principally manufactured by the Forestville Manufacturing Company around 1840.

Other manufacturers of the old timer clocks—pillar and scroll, looking glass, transition, and OG—include E. Terry & Sons; Mark Leavenworth; Eli Terry; Samuel Terry; Eli Terry & Son; Mitchell, Atkins & Company; Austin Chittenden; Marsh, Gilbert & Company; Jerome, Darrow & Company; and Eli Terry Junior as well as Seth Thomas.

Eli Terry patented the pillar-and-scroll clock, probably America's first mass-produced clock, in 1816. It evolved from his plain box case and had 30-hour wooden works. Other makers varied the case somewhat so they could copy the idea without infringing on Terry's patent.

Eli Terry (1772-1852) has earned the reputation as "The Father of the Clock Making Industry." His clock making career started in 1793 and spanned 60 years. He introduced ways that changed American clock making from handcrafting to manufacturing. Some of the clocks he made included wooden tall clocks, wooden shelf clocks and a variety of brass clocks. His name is still known and respected in the clock making industry today. Eli Terry's development of the wooden shelf clock contributed to the growth of his business. The old-fashioned tall clocks were losing popularity. One reason for this was that they were difficult to transport. A shelf clock, however, being considerably smaller, was easily transported and could be readily moved from room to room in family homes.

During the period between 1820 and 1840, Connecticut clock makers were busy making wooden shelf clocks. Brass shelf clocks were a thing of the future. These brass clocks were more costly to make than the wooden varieties. In some cases they were three times more expensive. However, many clock companies developed an interest in the cheap brass movement clock. Prior to the American Civil War, spring driven clocks came into vogue. After the American Civil War, expensive brass springs were replaced by steel springs. Shelf clocks with wooden works usually contain thirty-hour movements. Eight-day examples are unusual.

One competitor of Terry's was Joseph Ives, who began to make brass clocks in 1818. Chauncey Boardman (1789-1857) also became interested in the manufacture of shelf clocks.

The looking-glass clock had a mirror tablet instead of the usual picture or design. Thrifty housewives liked the combination clock-mirror. Chauncey Jerome claimed it as his idea even though his "bronze looking glass clock" with its bronze-colored pilasters, which gave it its name, was patented about three years after Joseph Ives patented a looking-glass clock in 1822.

Transition was the name given to certain clocks in the late 1820s, most of which had 30-hour weight-driven movements. They were carved or stenciled and had feet, frequently of the paw type. Often there were side columns, and a stenciled or carved top slat that might be included. They were an in-between style, appearing about the time the pillar-and-scroll was high in popularity and the OG was new.

The OG (ogee) clock was a continuous favorite from around 1825 until 1920. Its box frame featured an OG (S-curved) veneered (usually mahogany) door molding and front. It had a decorated tablet. Early one-day weight driven examples were approximately 26 inches high to accommodate the falling weights, whereas the eight-day type usually measured about 34 inches high. Later, 15- or 16-inch high spring-driven, thirty hour miniature OG clocks became available.

During this time, the following companies represented the wide range of OG clock manufacturers who were reaping profits through the sale of this popular clock:

Manufacturer	Location
Ansonia Clock Company	Ansonia
Boardmen and Wells	Bristol
Brewster and Ingrahams	Bristol
Forestville Mfg. Company	Bristol
C. (Chauncey) Jerome	Bristol
Jerome and Company	New Haven
Manross, Pritchard and Co.	Bristol
Seth Thomas	Plymouth
Seth Thomas	Thomaston
Smith and Goodrich	Bristol
Smith and Brothers	New York City
Henry Terry	Plymouth
Terry and Andrews	Bristol
Waterbury Clock Company	Waterbury
E. N. Welch Mfg. Company	Bristol
Riley Whiting	Winchester

The following shows the exact words found on the backboard label of a Seth Thomas time-and-strike shelf clock with an alarm. The clock which was named after the town, Plymouth Hollow, was changed to Thomaston in 1866.

Thirty-Hour Spring Clocks
Seth Thomas
Thomaston, Conn.
Warranted Good

Directions for setting the clock running. Place the clock in a perpendicular position. Oil the pattetes or ends of the part commonly called the VERGE; the pin on which the verge plays, and the wire, which carries the pendulum, at the place where it touches the rod. One drop is sufficient for the whole. Hang on the pendulum ball, then put on key with handle down, and turn toward the figure VI and turn steadily until the clock is wound.

If the Clock should go too fast, lower the ball by means of a screw at the bottom of the pendulum; if too slow raise it.

If the hands want moving, do it by means of the longest, turning it at any time forward, but never backward, when the Clock is within fifteen minutes of striking; and in no case further than to carry the minute hand to the figure XII.

Should the Clock by any means strike wrong, it may be made to strike right by raising the small wire hanging near the bell.

E. Howard & Company mahogany banjo wall clock with hand carved wooden ball and eagle at crest, circa 1880, eight-day, time only, weight driven, 10" wide at base, 39" high, 7" dial; $2,000.

Ansonia "Girandole" mahogany banjo wall clock with Westminster chimes, brass sidearms, and cut glass on throat and on round beveled glass door at base, eight-day, time and strike, spring driven, 12" diameter at base, 39" high, 8" dial; $2,500.

E. Ingraham "Nyanza" walnut stained banjo wall clock, circa 1917, eight-day, time and strike, 10" wide at base, 38" high; $425.

New Haven walnut banjo wall clock, circa 1895, beveled glass with New Haven on dial, time only, 25" high; $185.

Sessions banjo wall clock with brass eagle and sidearms, circa 1880, eight-day, time only; 12-1/2" wide at base, 42" high; $425.

New Haven "Whitney" banjo wall clock with sidearms and eagle crown, eight-day, time and strike, 10" wide at base, 32" high; $425.

Waltham mahogany banjo wall clock, in the Willard style, circa 1929, ivory enamel dial, Perry's Victory on glass tablet, weight driven, 10-1/2" wide, 41" high; $2,500.

Waterbury mahogany banjo wall clock with porcelain face, brass sidearms, circa 1908, eight-day, time only, weight driven, 10" wide at base, 42" high; $1,000.

Ithaca oak floor clock (grandfather clock), circa 1920, eight-day, time and strike, spring driven, 18" wide, 11" deep, 82" high; $750.

Rich & Holt oak grandfather clock (case made in America), circa 1920, 30-hour, strikes hour on cast iron bell (English made movement), 19" wide at top, 82" high; $1,750.

Seth Thomas mahogany custom made "grandfather look" floor clock, with OG upper section sitting on top of lower storage section, 30-hour, 19" wide, 77-1/2" high; $700.

View of Seth Thomas "grandfather look" clock with bottom door closed.

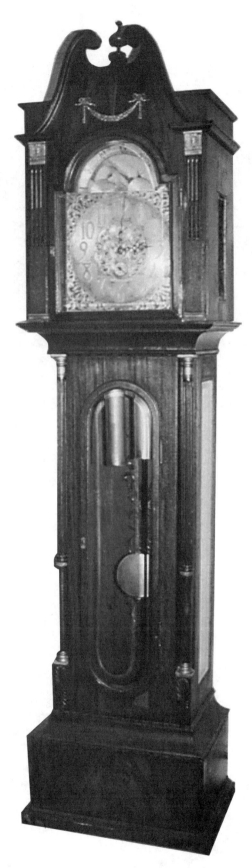

Waltham Clock Co, mahogany grandfather clock, made from a kit, early 1900s, brass weights and pendulum, beveled glass, applied brass decorations, moon dial, 91" high; $1,500.

Waterbury oak jeweler's regulator floor clock, eight-day, time only, weight driven, 31" wide, 13" deep, 105-1/2" high; $8,000.

J. C. Brown rosewood oversized OG, circa 1855, eight-day, time, strike, and alarm, 16-1/2" wide, 31" high; $350.

J. C. Brown rosewood wall hanging OG, 30-hour, time and strike, reverse painting on tablet, 15-1/2" wide, 25-1/2" high; $325.

Forestville Mfg. Co. mahogany OG, circa 1848, made by J.C. Brown, circa 1848, eight-day time and strike, weight driven, 17" wide, 29" high; $550.

Chauncey Jerome mahogany OG, circa 1845, replaced picture on tablet, 15-1/2" wide, 26" high; $300.

William S. Johnson rosewood miniature double OG shelf clock, circa 1860, 30-hour, 12" wide, 18-1/2" high; $225.

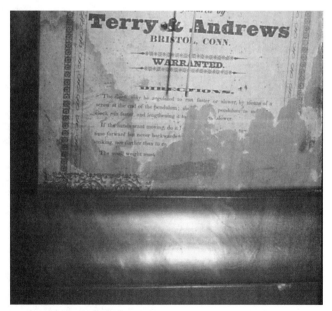

Label of Terry & Andrews OG shelf clock. It reads in part: "Manufactured by Terry & Andrews, Bristol, Conn. Warranted."

Terry & Andrews mahogany OG shelf clock, circa 1848, 30-hour, time and strike with wooden dial. Terry and Andrews were in business two years and helped found the Ansonia Clock Company, 15" wide, 26" high; $300.

Seth Thomas miniature OG mahogany shelf clock, after 1865, 30-hour, time, strike, and alarm, 10" wide, 16" high; $100.

Seth Thomas miniature OG mahogany shelf clock, after 1865, 30-hour, time and strike, 11" wide, 16-1/2" high; $150.

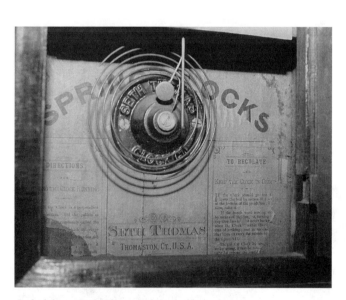

Label from Seth Thomas OG shelf clock.

Seth Thomas miniature OG rosewood shelf clock, after 1865, 30-hour, time and strike, spring driven, 10-1/2" wide, 16-1/2" high; $275.

Seth Thomas miniature OG mahogany simple calendar shelf clock with Seem's dial patented January 7, 1868, 30-hour, time and strike, spring driven, 12" wide, 18" high, no price available. Seth Thomas mirror OG mahogany simple calendar shelf clock with Seem's dial patented January 7, 1868, 30-hour, time and strike, weight driven, 15-1/2" wide, 26" high; no price available.

Close-up of dial from Seth Thomas simple calendar shelf clock marked "Seem's dial Patented January 7, 1868."

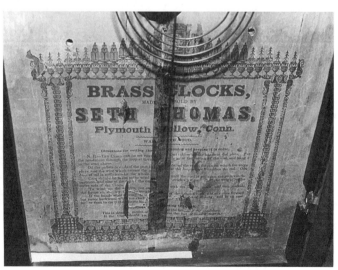

Label from Seth Thomas simple calendar shelf clock.

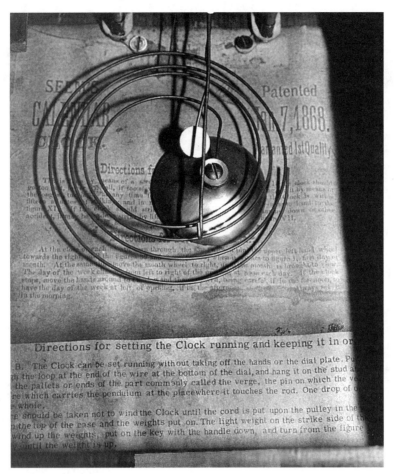

Seem's label from Seth Thomas simple calendar shelf clock.

Seth Thomas mahogany miniature mirror round band OG, 30-hour, time, strike and alarm, 11" wide, 16-1/2 " high; $185.

Seth Thomas rosewood OG made in Plymouth Hollow, circa 1860, eight-day time and strike, weight driven, 15-1/2" wide, 25-1/2" high; $200.

Seth Thomas rosewood miniature, round band OG, circa 1880, 30-hour time and strike, 10-1/2" wide, 16-1/2" high; $250.

Seth Thomas rosewood double OG, eight-day, time and strike, weight driven, 15" wide, 25-1/2" high; $450.

Label from Seth Thomas OG shelf clock. It reads, "Eight Day Weight Clocks, Seth Thomas, Thomaston, Conn., Warranted Good."

Seth Thomas rosewood round band OG, circa 1885, eight-day, time and strike, weight driven, 15" wide, 25" high; $450.

Seth Thomas miniature OG mahogany shelf clock (left), after 1865, eight-day, time and strike, 10-1/2 "wide, 16-1/2" high; $175. Seth Thomas miniature OG mahogany veneered shelf clock with S and T on hands for Seth Thomas, after 1865, 30-hour, time and strike, 10" wide, 16" high; $225.

E. N. Welch OG rosewood shelf clock, circa 1850, eight-day, time and strike, spring driven, 11-1/2" wide, 18-1/2" high; $350.

E. N. Welch rosewood OG, circa 1875, 30-hour, time and strike, 15" wide, 26" high; $300.

Label from E.N. Welch OG shelf clock. It reads, "Improved 30-Hour Brass Clocks Made and Sold By E. N. Welch Mfg. Co., Forestville, Conn., Warranted Good."

Seth Thomas rosewood flattop shelf clock, side columns, circa 1848, marked Plymouth Hollow, 30-hour, time only, 25" high; $240.

Seth Thomas mahogany pillar mirror shelf clock with Seth Thomas on the dial, time and strike, 10-1/2" wide, 16-1/2" high; $165.

Unknown maker, mahogany veneered mirror (replace) shelf clock, wooden works, 30-hour, time and strike, weight driven; 16-1/2" wide, 35-1/2" high; $450.

Unknown maker, mahogany shelf clock with stencil top and side columns, wooden movement and dial, 30-hour, time and strike, 32" high; $300.

Unknown maker, mahogany shelf clock, wooden dial, side columns, replaced decoration and panels, eight-day, time and strike, weight driven, label in clock give partial makers' names as "—ge and Fuller" – probably Birge and Fuller, 17-1/2" wide, 33" high; $450.

Unknown maker, mahogany shelf clock, side columns, time and strike, weight driven, label in clock names Covington, Indian and lists the makers as "Arwood & Cor—"; $250.

Seth Thomas (Plymouth Hollow) rosewood wall clock, 1850-1863, with cornice and columns, original tablets with reverse painting, eight-day, time and strike, weight driven, 16-1/2" wide, 32" high; $600.

Chapter 7

Wall Clocks

Many of the earliest wall clocks for use in schools, offices and churches originated in Connecticut. Octagon clocks were frequently referred to as "schoolhouse clocks." They were also popular in large workplaces or factories to keep employees informed of the time. The large round dial gallery clocks, most commonly found in eight-day examples, could be easily read because of their size. These latter clocks have been made since 1845.

An extremely useful wall clock was the regulator. Because of its split second accuracy, it was used in jewelry store windows where passersby could check to see whether their watches were running correctly. Railroad stations also used regulators to make sure trains ran on schedule. Their accuracy enabled them to be used for the regulation of other timekeepers. As time passed, however, a great number of clocks called regulators, or those with this name on their tablets, were not accurate enough to be so named. "Regulator" had just become a generic term for a hanging wall clock.

Two companies, Edward P. Baird of Plattsburgh, New York, and The Sidney Advertiser were active in the manufacture of advertising clocks. From around 1895-1900 Baird made wooden advertising clocks that had embossed or painted ads encircling the dial. The Sidney Company used sound devices in their clocks. For example, one clock had a bell that rang and advertising drums that turned every five minutes.

"Wag-on-Wall" clocks produced by Waterbury were a series of oak hanging study clocks, either weight or spring driven. Waterbury called these "study clocks" and used numbers to identify them. "Wag-on-Wall" clocks were sold without a case and were the earliest wall clock made. Gideon Roberts (1749-1813) made an all-wooden "wag-on-wall" in the late 1700s. Metal plates enclosed the movement but the exposed pendulum swung below the clock's body.

In an early 1900 catalog, the Ansonia Clock Company featured wall regulators named after the following female regents: Queen Anne, Queen Charlotte, Queen Elizabeth, Queen Isabelle, Queen Jane, Queen Mab, Queen Mary and Queen Victoria. These clocks were eight-day strikers with eight-inch dials and averaged between 37 to 42 inches in height. The woods available for their cases were black walnut, mahogany, or oak. All of the clocks except the Queen Mary were available in the popular oak. The individual purchase price for these clocks was well under $20.

Wall clocks were occasionally found in the Mission-style, which were made of oak and had straight, sturdy lines. They remained in style from the turn of the century until the late 1920s. The 1960s showed a rebirth of mission furniture and reproductions in that style.

Although calendar clocks did not appear until the mid-1800s, a calendar movement was put in a tall case clock in England in 1660. Almost two hundred years later, in 1853, J. H. Hawes of Ithaca, New York, was the first known American to patent a simple calendar clock mechanism. The Ithaca Calendar Clock Company, formed in 1865, used Henry B. Horten's perpetual roller-type calendar clock patent.

The difference between a perpetual calendar clock and a simple calendar clock is how they account for the days in a year. The perpetual clock indicates the day of the week, the month, and the date. It is self-adjusting to allow for leap year. The simple calendar clock requires an occasional manual adjustment to make it accurate.

The Waterbury perpetual calendar clocks could be furnished with languages other than English. Spanish, Portuguese, French, German, Swedish, and Italian calendar clocks became available in 1881.

One of the clock makers who developed a calendar dial was Charles W. Feishtinger. The dial showed the day of the week, the month, and the date of the month. A sweep hand marked the dates, which circled the dial. In the middle of the main dial, a short hand marked the month. A rectangular window beneath the month dial indicated the days. The movement and the case that was used for this clock was supplied by the Waterbury Clock Company.

Appendages on wall clocks were influenced by the furnishing style of the Victorian Era, named after England's Queen Victoria who reigned from 1837 to 1901. In the later half of the 1800s, both drop and upright carved finals, curved moldings and carvings, including heads, were used on clocks as well as furniture. Incised carving prevailed around 1870. Although oak and mahogany were occasionally used for clock cases, walnut was the clock maker's choice.

The pendulum is one thing wall clocks have in common. The pendulum is a clock weight, often ornamental, that hangs from a fixed point so it can swing to and fro as it regulates the clock's movement. Brooks Palmer, in his book *The Book of American Clocks*, reminds readers that the term "bob" is commonly used but incorrectly defined. He points out that a pendulum "has three parts—the pendulum rod and the pendulum ball, which most people call the bob, and the real bob which is the wire loop threaded for the regulating nut."

The weight at the end of the pendulum rod is called the ball or the bob. It is often ornamental as well as necessary. Its shape may be geometrical or round and can be fitted with decorative appendages. Examples include either a man's head or a woman's head in low relief Often times crystal, sandwich glass and wooden examples are found. Although genuine mercury pendulum bobs were found on French clocks, imitation mercury was used on American examples. The first man to create a practical pendulum was Christaan Huygens in about 1657. Before this invention, Galileo (1564-1642) thought that a pendulum was possible after comparing the similarity between it and a swinging lamp.

Bulova electric wall clock, 16" wide, 16" high; $110.

Baird advertising wall clock, circa 1896, eight-day, time only, spring driven, 31" high; $1,500.

W. L. Gilbert dark stained wall clock advertising Sauer's Extracts; glass etched and coins are gold leafed, eight-day, time only, spring driven, 40" high; $2,750.

Hammond Clock Company metal case Postal Telegraph "Synchronous Electric Time" gallery wall clock, circa 1931, 15" dial; $75.

E. Ingraham oak simple calendar clock, "Josephson, the Quality Jewelry Store" on lower tablet, eight-day, time only, spring driven, 16" wide, 36" high, 11" dial; $450.

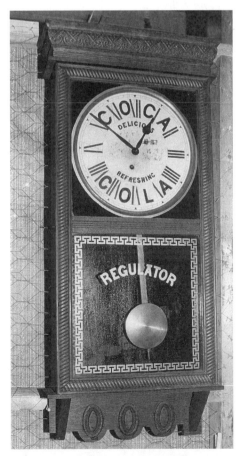

E. Ingraham oak advertising wall clock, circa 1900, "Coca Cola, Delicious, Refreshing" on dial, eight-day, time only, 17" wide, 38" high; $450.

Ithaca Calendar Clock Company "Belgrade" walnut per-petual calendar wall clock, patented 1866, wooden bob and provisions for the date, day and month on the lower tablet, W.H. Kelley Jewelry on dial, eight-day, time and strike, 14" wide, 38" high; $3,200.

Sessions walnut stained La Reforma advertising wall clock with repainted tablet, circa 1903, eight-day, time only, spring driven, 16-1/2" wide, 38" high; $595.

Waterbury "Orient" square top, short-drop jeweler's wall clock, eight-day, time only, spring driven, 10" wide at base, 15" wide at top, 27" high, 9" dial; $550.

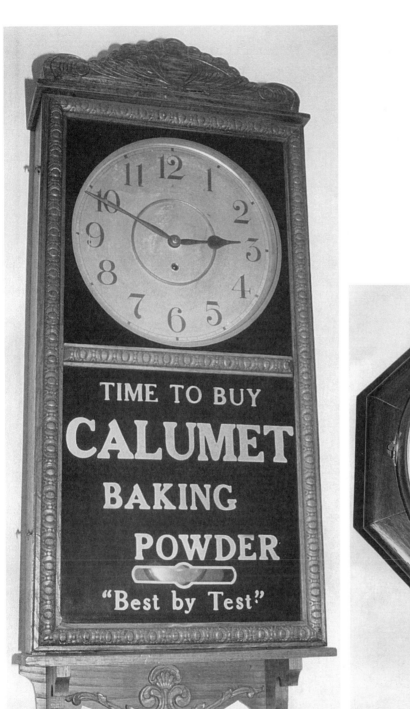

Waterbury oak advertising wall clock, "Calumet Baking Powder," repainted tablet, eight-day, time only, spring driven, 16" wide, 38" high; $595.

Waterbury oak octagon, short-drop advertising wall clock with reversed dial and hands that turn counterclockwise— often used in barbershops to reflect time in mirror, eight-day, time only, spring driven, 23" high, 11" dial; $800.

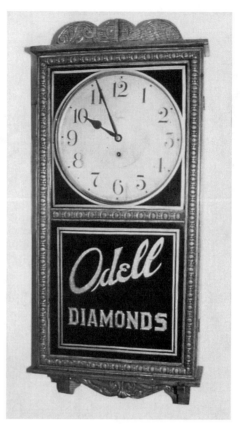

Waterbury oak Jeweler's regulator wall clock advertising Odell Jewelry Store, Quincy, Illinois, time only, 37" high; $650.

Waterbury oak round top, short-drop jeweler's wall clock, eight-day, time only, spring driven, advertising "T. W. Swan, Jeweler," 24" high, 11" dial; $600.

Waterbury oak store regulator with Coca-Cola advertisement on bottom tablet, time and strike (most of these are time only), top tablet is original but bottom is replaced, 16" wide, 36" high; $450.

Ansonia Brass and Copper Company "Novelty Calendar" mahogany veneered octagon, short-drop simple calendar clock, eight-day, time only, spring driven, 17" wide, 26" high, 10-1/2" dial; $1,250.

Ansonia Brass and Copper Company "Novelty Calendar" mahogany veneered octagon, short-drop simple calendar clock, exact copy case, eight-day, time only, spring driven, 17" wide, 26" high, 10-1/2" dial; $700 for copy, $1,000 for original.

Ansonia Brass & Copper Company rosewood veneered round top, short-drop perpetual calendar clock with W.A. Terry's calendar movement patents, 1868, 1870, and 1875; an exact copy of case and dial but with original works, eight-day, time and strike, 16" wide, 25-1/2" high, 11" dial; $500 for copy, $900 for original.

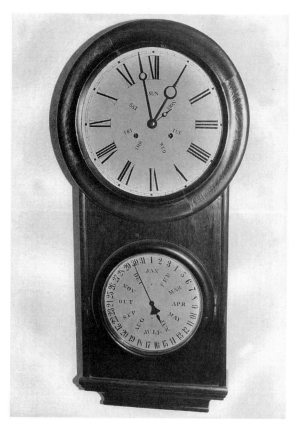

L.F. & W.W. Carter Clock Company, Bristol, Connecticut, rosewood round top, short-drop perpetual calendar clock with double dial, circa 1863-68, eight-day, time and strike, spring driven, 32" high, 11-1/2" dial, $1,300.

W.L. Gilbert "Berkshire" walnut simple calendar clock, circa 1870, eight-day, time and strike, spring driven, 14-1/2" wide, 38" high, 8" dial; $4,500.

W.L. Gilbert "Office" walnut simple calendar octagon wall clock, applied decorations, eight-day, time and strike, 32" high; $1,200.

W.L. Gilbert walnut round top short-drop simple calendar clock, early 1900s, eight-day, time and strike, spring driven, 18-1/2" wide, 31" high; $850.

E. Ingraham oak octagon short-drop simple calendar clock, circa 1900, eight-day, time only, spring driven, 17" wide, 24" high; $425.

E. Ingraham oak simple calendar octagon wall clock, circa 1910, face and tablet replaced with exact copy, eight-day, time only, 18" wide, 32" high; $425.

E. Ingraham Company walnut stained simple calendar wall clock with calendar dates on upper dial, eight-day, time only, 12" wide, 24" high; $525.

E. Ingraham stained walnut round top simple calendar clock, circa 1890, eight-day, time only, spring driven, 24" high, 11" dial; $400.

Ithaca Calendar Clock Company "Kildare" mahogany perpetual calendar wall clock, intricate case carving, sweep second hand and provisions for the date, day and month on the lower tablet, cut crystal bob, eight-day, time and strike, 13" wide, 33" high; $5,500.

Ithaca Calendar Company "Number 1" walnut perpetual calendar wall clock with H.B. Horton's patents, April 18, 1865, and Aug. 28, 1866, and provisions for the date, day and month on the lower tablet, sweep second hand, double weight driven, time only, 19" wide, 6 feet high; $15,000.

Ithaca "Number 4" walnut perpetual calendar clock with H.B. Horton's perpetual calendar movement patent 1865, eight-day, time and strike, double spring driven, 31" high, 12" diameter upper dial, 9" diameter lower dial; $1,500.

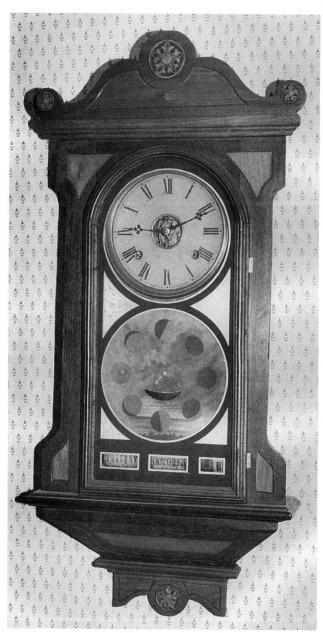

New Haven "Register" walnut double-dial perpetual calendar clock, eight-day, time only, spring driven, 12" wide, 33" high, 7" top dial, 7-1/2" bottom dial; $600.

Macomb Clock Company walnut perpetual calendar clock with double dial Seem's calendar and eight phases of the moon, movement by E.N. Welch, circa 1882-83, eight-day, time and strike, spring driven, 14-1/2" wide, 30" high, 6" dial; no price available.

New Haven oak simple calendar clock with double dial, 30-day, time only, spring driven, 19-1/2" wide, 48" high; $1,500.

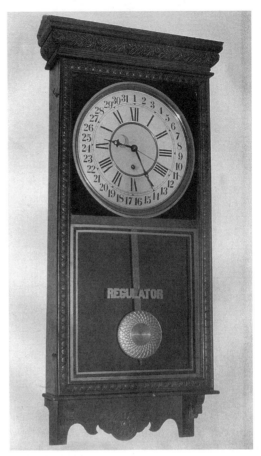

Sessions oak calendar clock, early 1900s, eight-day, time only, spring driven, 16-1/2" wide, 36" high; $500.

Sessions oak calendar clock, circa 1910-1920, eight-day, time only, spring driven, 16-1/2" wide, 38" high; $500.

Sessions walnut simple calendar wall clock, circa 1890, eight-day, time only, 39" high; $550.

Seth Thomas "Number 1" rosewood perpetual calendar wall clock, patented 1876, eight-day, time only, weight driven, 40" high; $3,500.

Seth Thomas "Number 5" walnut perpetual calendar wall clock with second hand, applied walnut decorations, calendar details found on lower dial, time only, weight driven, 50" high; $7,500.

Seth Thomas "Number 6-1/2" rosewood veneered double-dial perpetual calendar clock, calendar movement patented February 15, 1876, eight-day, time only, spring driven, 32" high, 11-1/2" top dial, 9-1/2" bottom dial; $1,500.

Seth Thomas "Office Number 11" mahogany perpetual calendar wall clock, patented 1876, eight-day time only, weight driven, 68-1/2" high: $17,500.

E.N. Welch "Damrosch" walnut perpetual calendar clock with double dial, eight-day, time only, spring driven, 14" wide, 41" high, 8" dials; $2,400.

E.N. Welch "Number 1" rosewood veneered calendar clock with double dial, an exact copy of case and dials but with original works, eight-day, time only, 16-1/2" wide, 54-1/2" high; $1,000 for copy, $2,700 for original.

E.N. Welch oak veneered octagon, short-drop simple calendar clock, dated 1887, eight-day, time and strike, spring driven, 17" wide, 24" high; $500.

E.N. Welch walnut perpetual calendar clock, an exact copy of case and dials but with original works, Daniel J. Gale Astronomical Calendar clock patents, 1871, 1877, and 1885, eight-day, time and strike, spring drive, 17" wide, 30" high, 11" dial; $1,500 for copy, $4,000 for original clock.

E.N. Welch oak simple calendar wall clock, circa 1890, eight-day, time only, 18" wide, 40" high; $695.

Welch, Spring & Co. "Calendar Number 1" rosewood round top, long-drop double-dial calendar clock, circa 1868-84, with B.B. Lewis type calendar dial, eight-day, time only, weight driven, 18" wide, 52-1/2" high, $2,250.

Welch, Spring & Co. "Number 2" rosewood perpetual calendar wall clock with provisions on the upper dial for the days of the week marked by a small hand and on the lower dial for the days indicated by a large hands and the months marked with a small hand, Lewis patented calendar mechanism, eight-day, time only, 13" wide, 34" high; $1,600.

A close-up of B.B. Lewis's Perpetual Calendar label patented Feb. 4, 1862, Sept. 15, 1863, June 21, 1864 and Dec. 20, 1864, on the Welch, Spring & Co. Calendar clock.

E. Ingraham gallery clock, circa 1900, time only, spring driven, 16" diameter; $900.

Samuel Emerson Root metal wall clock with case made by Nicholas Muller, circa 1850, eight-day, time only, marine movement, 12" diameter, 5" dial, no price available.

Seth Thomas walnut gallery clock, 15-day, time only, 18" dial, 25-1/2" outside diameter; $2,500.

Seth Thomas metal case gallery clock, 30-day, time only, spring driven, 22" diameter, 13" dial; $900.

Seth Thomas oak gallery clock, 30-day, time only, 20" diameter, 17" dial, $900.

Waterbury oak gallery clock, 30-day, time only, spring driven, 30" diameter, 23" dial; $2,000.

Unknown maker, Mission-style oak wall clock, eight-day, time and strike, spring driven, 12-1/2" Square; $100.

Unknown maker, Mission-style oak wall clock, eight-day, time and strike, spring driven, 12-1/2" wide, 26" high; $150.

Ansonia "Regulator A" walnut octagonal wall clock, circa 1900, with ebony trim, eight-day, time and strike, 17" wide, 32" high; $500.

Ansonia oak, "Regulator B" drop octagon clock, circa 1890, time only, 17" wide, 32" high; $450.

Ansonia oak miniature octagonal wall clock, circa 1910, time and strike, 12" wide, 20" high; $225.

E. Ingraham oak octagon, short-drop wall clock, eight-day, time only, spring driven, 18" wide, 24" high; $325.

E. Ingraham octagon short-drop regulator, early 1900s, eight-day, time only, spring driven, 24-1/2" high; 11-1/2" dial, $275.

W.L. Gilbert rosewood veneered octagon short-drop wall clock, eight-day, time only, 21" high, 7-1/2" dial; $300.

New Haven walnut veneered octagon short-drop wall clock, patented June 13, 1871, eight-day, time and strike, spring driven, 17" wide, 24" high; $400.

Sessions oak octagon, short-drop wall clock, circa 1903, eight-day, time only, spring driven, 24" high, 10" dial; $275.

Seth Thomas "Number 3" walnut octagon, long-drop wall clock, second hand, "Ball Watch Co., Cleveland" on dial, time only, weight driven, 14" dial, 44" high; $4,200.

Seth Thomas oak octagon short-drop wall clock, eight-day, time only, spring driven, 17-1/2" high, 8" dial; $200.

Seth Thomas "Number 18" walnut octagon, long-drop wall clock, nickel-plated pendulum and weight, eight-day, time only, weight driven, 14" dial, 54" high; $4,000.

Seth Thomas walnut octagon, short-drop wall clock, circa 1900, eight-day, time only, spring driven, 21-1/2" high; $350.

Seth Thomas oak octagon, short-drop wall clock, with label reading "Union Pacific Railroad Company Station Clock", eight-day, time only, spring driven, 24" high; $375.

Unknown maker, mahogany veneered octagon, long-drop wall clock, eight-day, time and strike, spring driven, 31-1/2" high, 12" dial; $495.

Waterbury "Yeddo" rosewood veneered octagon, short-drop wall clock with brass trim, circa 1900, eight-day, time and strike, spring driven, 14" wide, 21-1/2" high, 10" dial; $325.

Waterbury "Yeddo" rosewood veneered octagon short-drop wall clock with brass trim, circa 1900, eight-day, time and strike, spring driven, 21" high, 10" dial; $395.

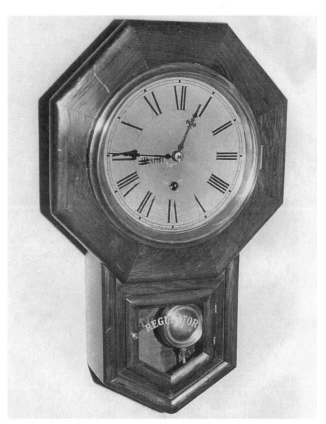

Waterbury octagon, short-drop wall clock, circa 1900, eight-day, time only, spring driven, 19" high, 7" dial; $350.

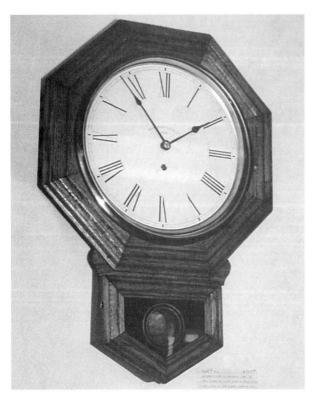

Waterbury oak octagonal wall clock, circa 1900, eight-day, time only, 17" wide, 24" high; $325.

E.N. Welch "Number 2" mahogany veneered octagon short-drop wall clock, circa 1880, eight-day, time only, spring driven, 17" wide, 25-1/2" high; $325.

E.N. Welch "Verdi" rosewood octagon long-drop wall clock, circa 1875, eight-day, time and strike, spring driven, 31" high; 11-1/2" dial; $500.

Close-up of label from E.N. Welch octagonal clock. The label reads, "Eight Day, Pendulum Octagon Clocks, Manufactured by the E.N. Welch Mfg. Co., Forestville, Conn., U.S.A. Designed for Offices, Halls, Depots, Schools—an article suited to any public place, and of quality not to be obtained elsewhere. A full supply, both silent and striking, constantly on hand."

E.N. Welch mahogany veneered octagon, short-drop wall clock, eight-day, time only, spring driven, 26" high, 11-1/2" dial; $325.

American Clock Company battery-operated birch wall clock, time only, 16" wide, 47" high, 11" dial; $550.

Ansonia walnut short-drop wall clock, 30-day, time only, 11" dial, 24" high; $350.

Ansonia "Antique Hanging" cherry wall clock, brass and porcelain dial, antique brass trimmings, eight-day, time and strike, weight driven, 46-1/2" high; $9,000.

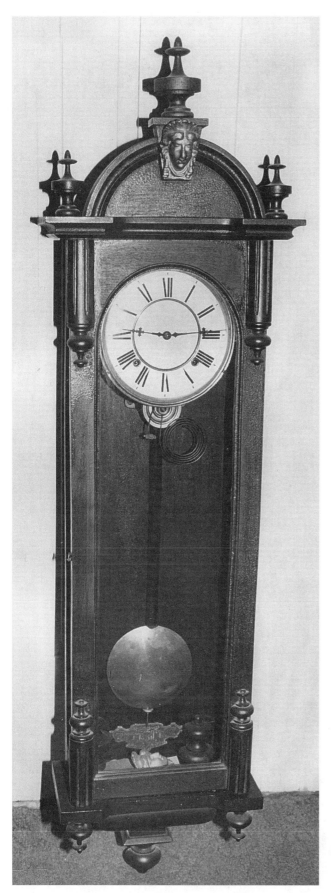

Ansonia "Charlotte" oak wall clock, eight-day, time and strike, spring driven, 16" wide, 41" high; $800.

Ansonia "Capitol" walnut wall clock, eight-day, time and strike, spring driven, 13-1/2" wide, 53" high, 7" dial; $1,500.

Ansonia "Queen Charlotte" oak wall clock, barley twist columns, pressed carving, eight-day, time only, 16" wide, 42" high; $800.

Ansonia "Queen Elizabeth" oak wall clock, awarded a prize medal at the Paris Exposition in 1878 as indicated by the label on the back of the case, eight-day, time and strike, 13-1/2" wide, 38" high; $950.

Ansonia "Queen Elizabeth" walnut wall clock, circa 1901, incised carving, eight-day, time only, 37" high; $600.

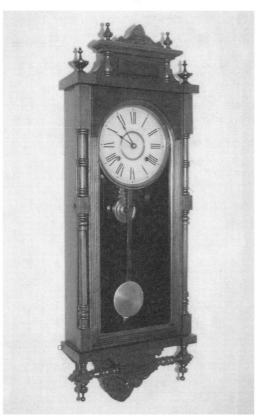

Ansonia "Queen Elizabeth" walnut wall clock, circa 1901, incised carving, eight-day, time and strike, 37" high; $700.

Ansonia reflector ebony finished wall clock with Mary Gregory type etching on tablet, circa 1880, eight-day, time and strike, spring driven, 14" wide, 35" high; $950.

Gustav Becker walnut wall clock, porcelain dial with brass surrounds, turned columns, time and strike, 16" wide, 33" high, runs about two weeks; no price available.

W.L. Gilbert "Columbia" walnut wall clock, circa 1886, incised carving, applied decorations, eight-day, time and strike, 17" wide, 36" high; $850.

Bundy Time Recorder walnut wall clock, incised carving, runs 15 days, 16" wide, 55" high. The Bundy movement was by Seth Thomas. Each employee had a key number; $3,500.

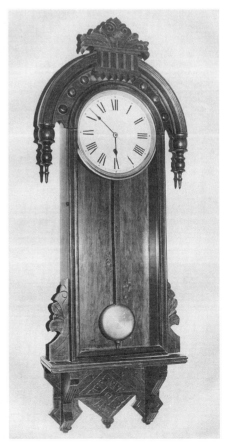

W.L. Gilbert "Gladstone" walnut wall clock, eight-day, time only, spring driven, 13" wide, 38" high, 7" dial; $600.

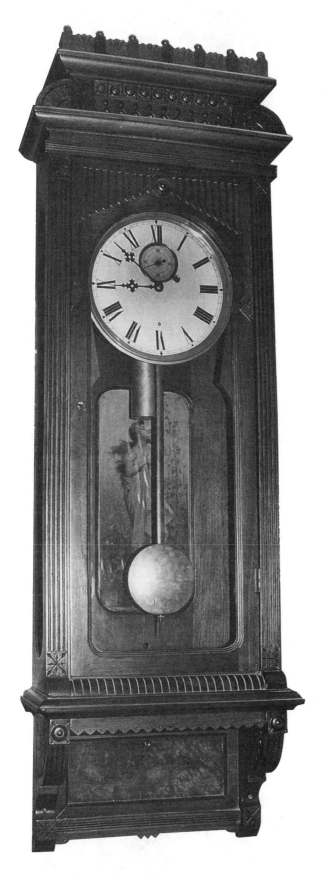

W.L. Gilbert "Number 10-1/2" walnut parlor wall regulator, circa 1888, eightday, time only, weight driven, 17-1/2" wide, 54" high; $2,200.

W.L. Gilbert "Number 10-1/2" oak wall clock, eight-day, time only, weight driven, 16" wide, 53" high; $2,200.

W.L. Gilbert Clock Company "Number 11 Regulator" walnut wall clock, circa 1888, eight-day, time and strike, weight driven with keyhole on right that winds both weights on same drum, 14-1/2" wide, 50" high, 7" dial; $1,500.

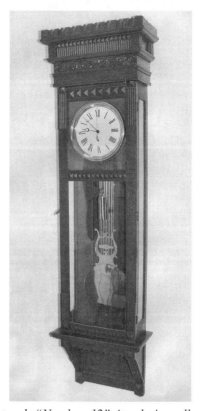

W.L. Gilbert "Number 11" ash parlor wall regulator, circa 1888, eight-day, time and strike, weight driven, 15" wide, 50" high, 8" dial; $2,200.

W.L. Gilbert oak "Number 12" jeweler's wall regulator, early 1900s, eightday, time only, weight driven, 30" wide, 84" high; $7,000.

W.L. Gilbert "Observatory" oak regulator wall clock, circa 1910, pressed designs and incised carving, eight-day, time only, 15-1/2" wide, 34" high; $400.

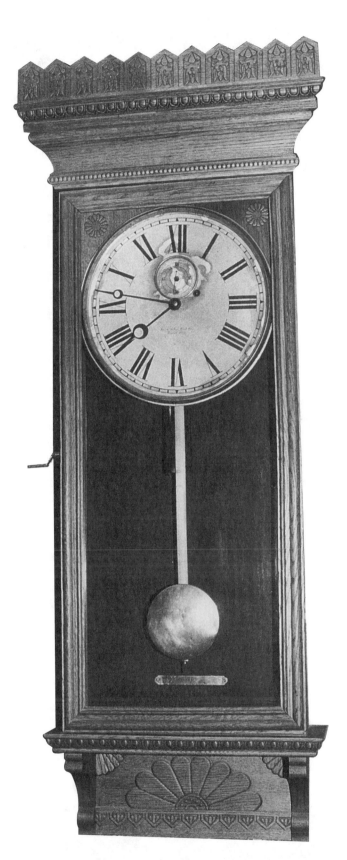

W.L. Gilbert "Number 14" oak parlor wall regulator, eight-day, time only, weight driven, 17" wide, 49" high; $2,000.

W.L. Gilbert "Shield" walnut wall clock, circa 1881, eight-day, time and strike, spring driven, 10-1/2" wide, 29" high, 6" dial; $950.

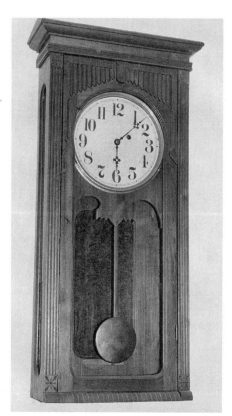

W.L. Gilbert walnut wall clock with pediment missing, circa 1890, eight-day, time only weight driven, 15-1/2" wide, 37" high, 9-1/2" dial; $450.

W. L. Gilbert oak parlor wall regulator, time only, 13-1/2" wide, 36" high; $425.

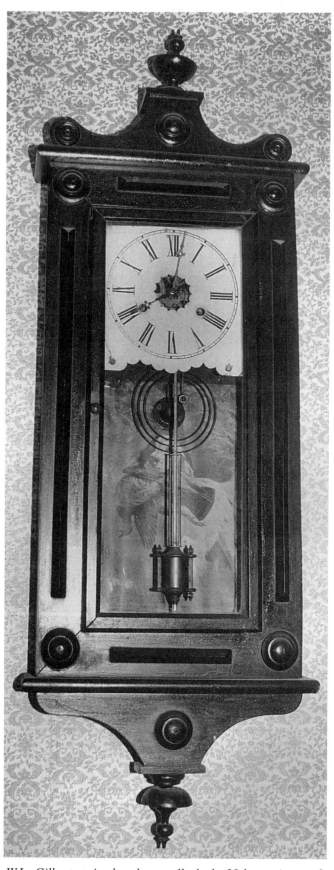

W.L. Gilbert stained walnut wall clock, 30-hour, time and strike, weight driven, 16" wide, 47" high; $400.

E. Ingraham "Mount Vernon" oak hanging shelf clock, circa 1880, eight-day, time and strike, spring driven, 14-1/2" wide, 27" high; 5" dial; $600.

E. Ingraham walnut hanging kitchen wall clock, circa 1893, incised carving, thermometer and level attached to clock, eight-day, time and strike, 28" high; $650.

E. Ingraham Company walnut ionic round top, round-drop wall clock, circa 1875, eight-day, time and strike, spring driven, 22" high, lower glass diameter 6", 10" dial, $350.

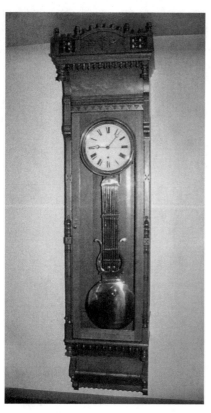

F. Kroeber "Jeweler's Regulator Number 58" brass lyre pendulum, sweep second hand, eight-day, time only, pinwheel escapement (more desirable than the dead-beat), 22" wide, 93" high; $15,000.

F. Kroeber walnut regulator wall clock, circa 1898, turned and reeded columns, sweep second hand, time only, weight driven, 53" high; $3,000.

C.H. Maur wall clock, painted porcelain dial, ormolu face and hands, 15-jewel clock with platform escapement, time only, 8" wide, 6-1/2" high; $900.

New Haven "Office Number 1" walnut regulator wall clock, circa 1886, second hand, time only, single weight driven, 42" high; $1,200.

New Haven "Pacific" oak wall clock, circa 1880, eight-day, time only, spring driven, 16-1/2" wide, 38" high; $500.

New Haven oak parlor wall regulator, early 1900s, time only, spring driven, 16" wide, 45" high; $450.

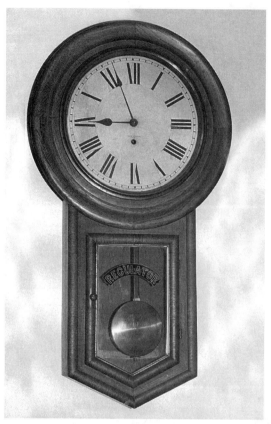

New Haven mahogany round top, long-drop regulator, eight-day, time only, spring driven, 32" high, 12" dial; $400.

New Haven walnut round top, short-drop regulator, eight-day, time and strike, spring driven, 16" wide, 28" high; $425.

New Haven pine stained round top, short-drop wall clock, eight-day, time only, 14-1/2" high, 4-1/2" dial; $150.

New Haven oak wall clock, circa 1920, time and strike, chime rod rather than gong, 16" wide, 31" high; $475.

New Haven works in English walnut case with marquetry designs, eight-day, time and strike, spring driven, 38" high, 7-1/2" dial; $850.

New Haven mahogany wall clock, circa 1910, beveled glass, time and bimbam strike on two rods, 8" wide, 24" high; $275.

Schmid plastic case wall clock, circa 1950, time only, 14-1/2" high; $100.

New York Standard Watch Co. oak wall clock, patented Feb. 25, 1896, originally run by a dry cell battery, 20" wide, 48" high; $1,595.

Sessions "Regulator No. 5" walnut stained wall clock, circa 1895, incised carving, second hand, time only, double weight driven, 20" wide, 49" high; $3,700.

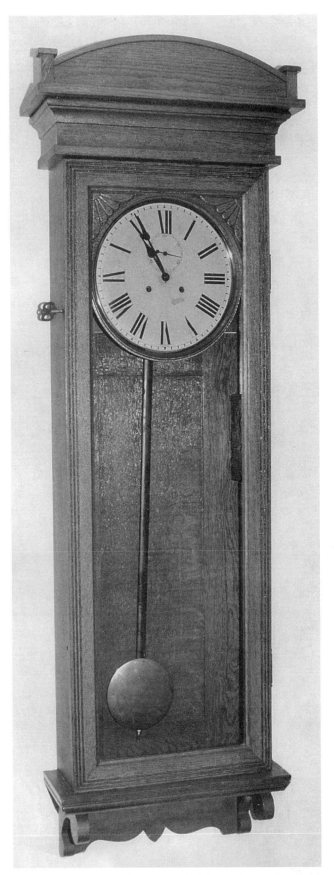

Sessions, oak wall clock, circa 1903, eight-day, time and strike, weight driven, 52" high, 12" dial; $1,000.

Sessions oak wall clock, circa 1903, eight-day, time and strike, weight driven with narrow flat weights to make them less discernible, 17" wide, 64" high, 11" dial; $1,350.

Sessions wall clock, eight-day, time and strike, spring driven, 19" high, 5" dial; $225.

Sessions oak parlor wall regulator, circa 1903, eight-day, time only, spring driven, 17" wide, 35" high; $375.

Seth Thomas "18 Inch Lobby" oak wall clock, second hand, incised carving, lever movement, 15-day, time only, 25" wide, 38" high; $2,500.

Seth Thomas "Eclipse" walnut wall clock, circa 1890, incised carving, eightday, time, strike, and alarm, Eclipse movement, 15" wide, 27" high; $600.

Seth Thomas "Flora" oak wall clock, flower carved on clock's side, hand carving on case, eight-day, time and strike, weight driven, 8" dial diameter, 38" high; $2,800.

Seth Thomas "Flora" walnut wall clock, circa 1880, incised designs and carving on side panel, eight-day, time and strike, weight driven, 13" wide, 38" high; $2,100.

Seth Thomas "Marcy" walnut wall clock, seen in 1884-1896 catalog, incised carving, eight-day, time and strike, spring driven, 8-1/2" diameter dial, 46" high; $5,000.

Seth Thomas "Number 1" rosewood regulator wall clock, circa 1855, round top, second hand, eight-day, time only, weight driven, 11" dial, 34" high; $2,250.

Seth Thomas "Number I Extra" Plymouth Hollow, Connecticut, rosewood parlor wall regulator, circa 1860, eight-day, time and strike, weight driven, 41" high, 13-1/2" dial; $2,800.

Seth Thomas "Number 2" walnut round top long-drop regulator, circa 1888, eight-day, time only, weight driven, 34" high, 12" dial; $1,400.

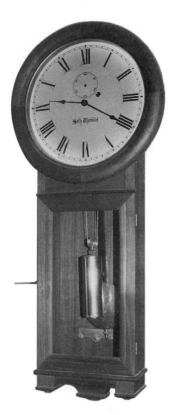

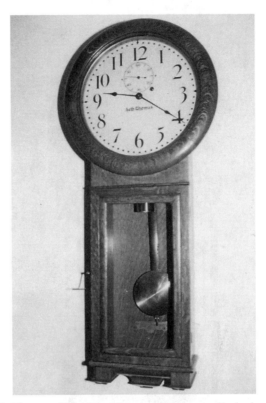

Seth Thomas "Number 2" walnut round top, long-drop regulator, eight-day, time only, weight driven, 10" wide, 35" high, 11-1/2" dial; $1,200.

Seth Thomas "Number 2" oak regulator wall clock, circa 1900, second hand, brass pendulum and weight, time only, weight driven, 10" wide, 36" high; $1,300.

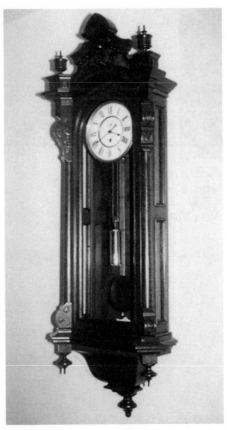

Seth Thomas "Regulator No. 5" walnut wall clock (also called "Miniature 16"), incised carving, glass sides, porcelain dial, eight-day, time only, weight driven, 50" high; $8,000.

Seth Thomas "Regulator No. 7" cherry wall clock, hand carved cabinet, Graham dead-beat escapement, cut steel pinion movement, second hand, eight-day, time only, weight driven, 12" dial; $9,000.

Seth Thomas "Regulator No. 6" walnut wall clock, second hand, brass weight and pendulum, eight-day, time only, 10" dial diameter, 49" high. The 1906 catalog lists this clock available in either mahogany or oak; $3,700.

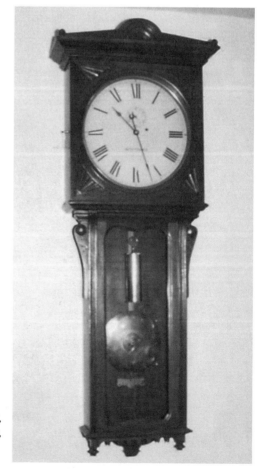

Seth Thomas "Regulator No. 8" cherry wall clock, second hand, brass weight and pendulum, eight-day, time only, 14" dial, 56" high; $8,500.

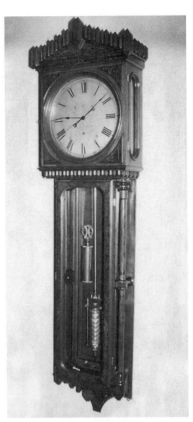

Seth Thomas "Fine Regulator No. 10" walnut wall clock, mercury pendulum, sweep second hand, turned side columns, burl decorations, glass sides in top section, 14" silver dial, eight-day, time only, 72" high. Some collectors consider this clock Thomas' best; $30,000.

Seth Thomas "Regulator No. 19" cherry wall clock, thumb spring mercury pendulum, sweep second hand, Graham dead-beat escapement, eight-day, time only, weight driven, 23" wide, 75" high; $22,000.

Seth Thomas "Regulator No. 19" walnut wall clock, incised carving, burl decorations, mercury pendulum, metal weight, Graham dead-beat escapement, second hand, eight-day, time only, 23" wide, 77" high; $20,000.

Seth Thomas "Regulator No. 30" oak wall clock, incised carving, applied decorations, time only, weight driven, 18" wide, 48" high; $2,200.

Seth Thomas "Number 60" mahogany regulator wall clock, brass pendulum and weight, eight-day, time only, weight driven, 18-1/4" wide, 60" high; $13,000. $15,000 if mint.

Seth Thomas "Number 60" mahogany wall clock, sweep second hand, brass weight, eight-day, time only, 14" dial, 58-1/2" high; $15,000.

Seth Thomas "Regulator No. 63" oak wall clock, circa 1900, applied decorations, beats seconds, Graham dead-beat escapement, eight-day, time only, weight driven, 14" dial, 76" high; $11,500.

Seth Thomas "Queen Ann" oak wall clock, pictured in 1881 catalog, eightday, time and strike, 13" wide, 36" high; $1,000.

Seth Thomas "Umbria" oak wall clock, 15-day, time only, double spring movement because of longer running time, 10" dial diameter, 40-1/2" high; $1,600.

Seth Thomas "Umbria" oak wall clock, second hand, brass pendulum, 15-day, time only, 40-1/2" high; $1,500.

Seth Thomas walnut hanging kitchen wall clock, circa 1890, incised carving, thermometer and level attached to clock, eight-day, time and strike, 30" high; $500.

Seth Thomas walnut hanging shelf clock, eight-day, time, strike, and alarm, spring driven, 15" wide, 27" high; $550.

Seth Thomas pine round top, long-drop regulator, eight-day, time only, weight driven, 33" high, 12" dial; $1,000.

Unknown maker, miniature school house type, dark stained wall clock, patented 1920, time only, spring driven, 5" dial, 14-1/2" high; $275.

Unknown maker, hanging Victorian wall clock, porcelain and brass dial, bird on clock's top, time only, 8" wide, 20" high; $350.

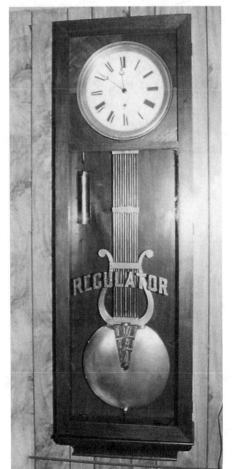

Unknown maker, American made cabinet, jeweler's regulator, circa 1840-1850, French works, walnut wall clock, pinwheel movement, time only, weight driven, 20" wide, 59" high; $1,250.

Waltham oak "16 Jewelers Regulator" wall clock, circa 1895, incised carving, time only, 18" wide, 67" high. This clock hung in a Davenport, Iowa jewelry store for 90 years; $3,700.

Waterbury "Alton" oak wall clock, eight-day, time and strike, spring driven, 16" wide, 39" high, 7" dial; $600.

Waterbury "Baha" gilded ionic wall clock, circa 1900, time and strike, 13" wide, 21" high; $375.

Waterbury "Cairo" oak wall clock, applied decorations, side columns, eight-day, time only, 17" wide, 42" high; $600.

Waterbury "Elgin" oak wall clock, eight-day, time only, spring driven, 15" wide, 33-1/2" high; $600.

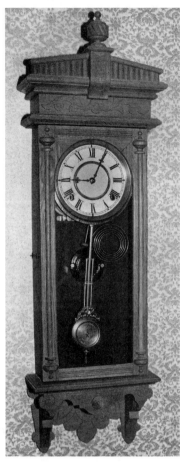

Waterbury "Halifax" oak wall clock, circa 1880, eight-day, time and strike, spring driven, 10" wide, 33" high; $600.

Waterbury "Library" mahogany wall clock, circa 1860, porcelain dial, eight-day, time and strike with chains that pull up weights, 17-1/2" wide, 41" high; $1,000.

Waterbury "Para" rosewood ionic wall clock, circa 1891, time only, 10" dial, 22" high; $375.

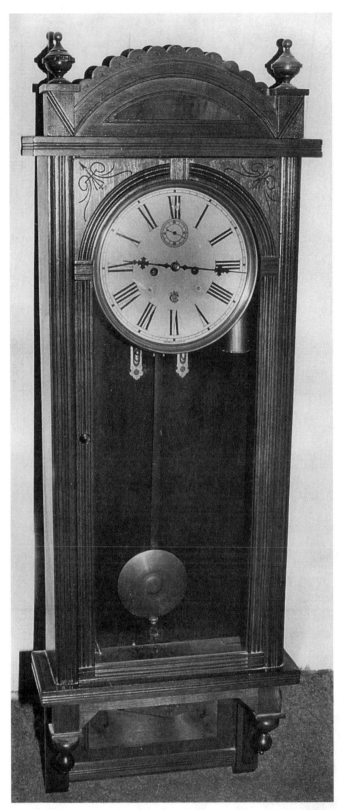

Waterbury cherry "Regulator No. 5" wall clock, burl decorations, incised carving, second hand, brass pendulum and weights, dead-beat escapement, second hand, glass sides, eight-day, time and strike, 19" wide, 68" high; $4,000.

Waterbury "Number 3" walnut parlor wall regulator, eight-day, time only, weight driven, 16" wide, 45" high, 8" dial; $1,600.

Waterbury "Number 53" walnut wall clock, circa 1900, eight-day, time only, weight driven, 20" wide at top, 53 -1/4" high, 9" dial; $1,500.

Waterbury "Regulator No. 53" mahogany wall clock, incised carving, lacy hands (common on Waterbury clocks), dead-beat escapement, eight-day, time only, double weight driven, 19-1/2" wide, 53" high; $3,500.

Waterbury "Saranac" oak hanging shelf clock, circa 1880, eight-day, time and strike, spring driven, 13-1/2" wide, 31" high, 5" dial; $600.

Waterbury "Union" walnut wall clock, pictured in its 1892 catalog, eight-day, spring driven; $500.

Waterbury walnut short drop wall clock, circa 1880-1890, time only, spring driven, 15" wide, 25" high; $325.

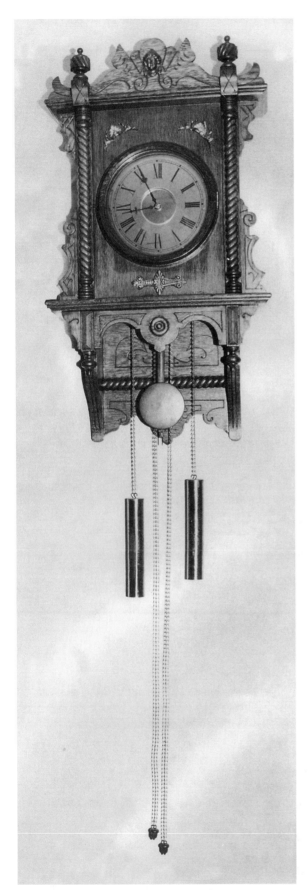

Waterbury two weight open swinger oak wall clock, circa 1880-1890, eight-day, time only, 17" wide, 30" high, 8" dial; $950.

Waterbury green painted round top, short-drop wall clock, eight-day, time only 13" high, 5" dial; $150.

E.N. Welch "Alexis Number 1" rosewood ionic wall clock, circa 1880, applied gold leaf on tablet, eight-day, time only, 12" dial, 26" high; $450.

E.N. Welch "Alexis Number 1" rosewood ionic wall clock, 30-day movement, time only, 12" dial, 26" high. The dial has been removed to show the works; $500.

A close-up of the label that reads, "Alexis Thirty Day, Time Piece, Patent Escapement."

Label on the back of E.N. Welch, "Eclipse" wall clock. It reads, "Eclipse manufactured exclusively for Metropolitan Mfg. Co."

E.N. Welch "Eclipse" manufactured for the Metropolitan Mfg. Co., walnut wall clock, incised carving, "Eclipse" pendulum, eight-day, time, strike and alarm, 14" wide, 27-1/2" high; $600.

E.N. Welch "Hanging Italian" rosewood veneer with walnut trim wall clock, sandwich glass insert in pendulum seen to the left of the case, eight-day, time and strike, 15" wide, 29" high; $900.

E.N. Welch "Italian" rosewood hanging shelf clock (new, exact copy case with original movement), eight-day, time and strike, spring driven, 15" wide, 29" high, 6" dial; $700 for copy, $1,500 for original.

E.N. Welch "Meyerbeer" oak regulator wall clock (Meyerbeer was an Italian composer who wrote Torchlight March No. 1 in B flat), circa 1885, eight-day, time and strike, 14" wide, 40" high; $750.

E.N. Welch "Number 2" rosewood round top, long-drop regulator, with exact copy case and original works, eight-day, time only, weight driven, 16" wide, 55" high, 18" dial; $2,000 for copy, $4,000 for original.

E.N. Welch, "No. 11 Regulator" mahogany wall clock, second hand, incised carving, 30-day, time only, spring driven, 18" wide, 60" high; $3,500.

E.N. Welch "No. 12 Regulator" walnut wall clock, incised carving, second hand, 30-day, time only, 23" wide, 65" high; $4,500.

E.N. Welch "Office Number 12" oak wall clock, circa 1885, incised carving, second hand, 30-day, time only, 23" wide, 65" high; $3,250.

E.N. Welch "Office 30-day" oak wall clock, circa 1900, incised carving, 30-day, time only, 18" wide, 60" high; $2,700.

E.N. Welch "Sembirch" walnut wall clock, circa 1890, incised carving, eight-day, time only, 14" wide, 39" high; $700.

E.N. Welch walnut wall clock (made exclusively for Metropolitan Mfg. Co., in New York), incised carving, painted dial, eight-day, time, strike and alarm, Eclipse pendulum, 14" wide, 27" high; $575.

E.N. Welch rosewood round top, long-drop wall clock, eight-day, time only, with two keyholes to wind weights, 35" high, 11-1/2" dial; $800.

E.N. Welch walnut hanging shelf clock, circa 1880, eight-day, time, strike and alarm, spring driven, 13-1/2" wide, 26" high; $450.

E.N. Welch oak wall clock with thermometer, circa 1880, eight-day, time only, lever movement, 23" high, 5-1/2" dial; $250.

Welch, Spring & Co. "Number 4 Regulator" walnut wall clock, 1873-1884, elaborately turned columns, upper finials, nickel-plated double spring movement, early model had wooden sides, later model had glass sides, 30-day time only, 16" wide, 42" high; $3,200.

Welch & Spring "No. 4 Regulator" walnut wall clock, circa 1880, turned columns, finials, dead-beat escapement, 30-day, time only, double spring driven, 16" wide, 41" high; $2,400.

Welch, Spring & Co. "No. 4 Regulator" walnut wall clock, brass pendulum, dead-beat escapement, 30-day, time only, double spring driven, 15" wide, 42" high; $1,900.

Welch, Spring & Co. rosewood "Number 6 Regulator" or "Lucca Regulator," 1879-1884, with two weights, movement has solid brass plates, lantern pinion and deadbeat escapement, eight-day, time only, 18-1/2" wide, 42" high; $7,200.

Welch & Spring "Number 6 Regulator" rosewood wall clock, circa 1868, eight-day, time only, double weight driven, 18" wide, 42" high; $8,000-9,000.

Chapter 8

Classic Clocks

In the ensuing chapter on classic clocks, we had originally included only three clock types—the crystal regulator, the porcelain shelf clock, and the statue or figural clock. We would like to add to the discussion some of the cabinet clocks by Ansonia Clock Company and F. Kroeber Clock Company.

All of the original figural clocks manufactured in the United States were produced by the Ansonia Clock Company and included "Arcadia," "Fortuna," "Gloria," and "Juno." They were eight-day, time-only, bronze-finished clocks with raised gold-plated numerals and ornamentation. Because there are known reproductions from European sources, buyers of these clocks should consult an expert to be sure the eventual purchase is not a reproduction.

Commanding high prices on today's market is the crystal regulator, a clock with glass panels on four sides, exposing the works to full view. Adding class to this clock are its visible or open escapement, porcelain dial, and beveled glass on the front, back, and side panels. These clocks range well over $3,000 in value.

W. L. Gilbert Clock Company produced an unusual crystal regulator, circa 1910, that stands on four fancy metal columns similar to an easel. The clock, finished in a rich ormolu gold, has a visible or open pendulum, ivory porcelain dial, and a visible escapement.

One of the most expensive crystal regulators put out by Ansonia Clock Company is the "Regal" clock as seen in their 1906 catalog. Finished in rich gold or Syrian Bronze, the "Regal" had an eight-day, half-hour gong striking movement, porcelain dial, visible or open escapement and beveled glass on all sides. Today this clock sells for well over $4,000.

In a catalog from 1902, W. L. Gilbert presented a crystal regulator, named "Verdi," that had an eight-day, half hour strike. It had an ivory dial, visible escapement, mercurial pendulum and front, side and back beveled glass panels. Finished in a rich, ormolu gold, the original cost was $60.

A later catalog by Gilbert featured a crystal regulator called "Magdeleine." The case was made of rich Brazilian onyx with round tapering onyx columns. The mountings were gold plate with heavy ornamental case decorations in rich ormolu gold-plate finish. It was priced at $100; for an additional $3 a lion ornament could be added to the top.

"Paris" was a crystal regulator manufactured by the Waterbury Clock Company. One of Waterbury's most expensive clocks of this type, the "Paris", sold for $50 in the early 1900s. Case finishes included gold-plate, Syrian bronze, polished brass and polished mahogany. Other characteristics included an ivory dial and visible or open escapement, with beveled-glass front, sides, and back panels. It also had a cast gilt bezel.

Two unique crystal regulators in Seth Thomas's Empire line were named "Empire No. 31" and "Empire No. 32." Each had a bronze-finished girl's head on top of the clock.

Ansonia's china or porcelain shelf clocks were hand painted with gold decorations. They had a rack strike, as well as a strike on the half hour with a cathedral striking gong on a sounding board. Features such as a cream porcelain dial and a rococo sash made these clocks extremely desirable. Germany's Royal Bonn Company manufactured many of the porcelain cases for these clocks. They were decorated in rich colors-green, ruby, turquoise, cobalt blue, and violet. Other features on these clocks included a French or rococo sash, beveled glass, porcelain visible escapement with a choice of an Arabic or a Roman dial. Ansonia Clock Company made the works for most of these clocks.

Clock advertisements used fancy phrases to depict a clock's charm. The following phrases from a catalog description exemplify this: "Assorted decorations, raised decorated flowers, Wedgewood decorations, rich color decorations, handpainted decorations, floral design, richly decorated and tinted cases."

Statue clocks are another of Ansonia's contribution to the clock industry's production of unique timepieces. The "Combatants" shows two war-like figures flanking the clock; "Music and Poetry" feature two female artists, one on each side of the clock; and "Pizarro and Cortez" is another example where two warriors flank the central clock.

Ansonia came out with a series of six cabinet clocks in the late 1800s, called "Cabinet A," "Cabinet D" "Cabinet F," "Senator," "Cabinet Antique," and "Cabinet No. 1". They were made of antique oak, mahogany, polished mahogany or polished oak with brass or ormolu trimmings. They ranged from 19 inches to 23 inches high. Today, the "Senator" is probably the most valuable. The case of this model is decorated with two antique brass female figures that flank the clock's dial.

Kroeber made more than fifty varieties of cabinet clocks. They are made of ebony, mahogany, walnut, or ash and have four and one-half or five-inch dials. These clocks are spring driven with eight-day time and strike and range in height from 13-1/2 to 18 inches. Kroeber's cabinet models date to the 1880s, and are described by number ("Cabinet No. 3," "Cabinet No. 4," etc.) rather than by name.

Ansonia "Admiral" polished mahogany crystal regulator, finished in rich gold, porcelain dial, mercury pendulum, open escapement, beveled glass, eight-day, time and half hour gong strike, 10" wide, 18" high; $4,000.

Ansonia "Apex" crystal regulator, finished in rich gold, porcelain dial, open escapement, beveled glass, eight-day, time and strike, 10" wide, 19" high; $3,600.

Ansonia "Floral" crystal regulator gold finish (catalog description) shelf clock, porcelain dial and open escapement, eight-day, time and strike, spring driven, 9" wide, 8" deep, 16" high; $1,250.

Ansonia "Regal" crystal regulator shelf clock, porcelain dial and open escapement, eight-day, time and strike, spring driven, 10-1/2" wide, 9" deep, 19" high; $4,500.

Ansonia crystal regulator with onyx top and base, visible (open) escapement, mercury pendulum, beveled plate glass, porcelain dial, eight-day, half hour gong strike, 10" wide, 17-1/4" high; $3,750.

Boston Clock Company "Alhambra" crystal regulator, patented Dec. 20, 1880, beveled glass, gold-plated case, 11-jeweled movement, porcelain dial, tandem wind movement, eight-day, time and strike, 14" wide, 23-1/2" high. When new cost was $133, now it is valued at $3,750.

Davies "Crystal Gem" mirror back shelf clock, patented March 23, 1875, eight-day, time and strike, spring driven, 16" high; $700. Davies wooden case shelf clock with warrior head on pendulum, eight-day, time and strike, spring driven, 16" high; $700.

Label from Davies "Crystal Gem" shelf clock

Seth Thomas "Empire Number 10" crystal regulator shelf clock, circa 1900, eight-day, time and strike, spring driven, 8" wide, 6-1/2" deep, 14-1/2" high; $700.

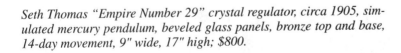

Seth Thomas "Empire Number 29" crystal regulator, circa 1905, simulated mercury pendulum, beveled glass panels, bronze top and base, 14-day movement, 9" wide, 17" high; $800.

Ansonia "La Charny" Royal Bonn porcelain shelf clock, porcelain dial, French sash bezel, eight-day, time and strike, 11" wide, 12" high; $675.

Ansonia "La Clair" Royal Bonn porcelain shelf clock, porcelain dial, rococo sash on door, circa 1890, eight-day, time and strike, 9-1/2" wide, 13" high; $650.

Ansonia "La Orne" Royal Bonn porcelain shelf clock, circa 1890, porcelain dial, eight-day, time and strike, 12" wide, 11" high; $650.

Ansonia Royal Bonn porcelain shelf clock with floral decorations on white case, circa 1890, eight-day, time and strike, spring driven, 10" wide, 12" high; $500.

Ansonia porcelain shelf clock (left to right) with blue and gold decorated case, patented June 18, 1882, by Tuckahoe China, eight-day, time and strike, spring driven, 9" wide, 11" high; $350. Ansonia Royal Bonn porcelain case, eight-day, time and strike, spring driven, 9-1/2" wide, 11-1/2" high; $425. Ansonia "Tally" porcelain shelf clock, circa 1900, eight-day, time and strike, spring driven; 9-1/2" wide, 10-1/2" high; $400.

Ansonia Dresden porcelain shelf clock; eight-day, time and strike, spring driven, 13" wide, 12" high, 4-1/2" dial; $550.

Close-up of Royal Bonn, Germany mark on Ansonia porcelain shelf clock.

Label from Ansonia Dresden porcelain shelf clock.

Ansonia Royal Bonn porcelain small case shelf clock with floral decorations, eight-day, time and strike, spring driven; 7-1/2" wide, 7" high; $450.

Ansonia Royal Bonn porcelain shelf clock, with porcelain dial and open escapement, eight-day, time and strike, spring driven, 10-1/2" wide, 11-1/2" high; $1,100.

Porcelain shelf clocks: left, Ansonia showing baby with clock; middle, German-made colored green and white; right, New Haven, colored green and white, circa 1900, 6" to 8" height range—$250 each.

W. L. Gilbert porcelain shelf clock with floral decorations on pale green case, circa 1890, eight-day, time and strike, spring driven, 9" wide, 10-1/2" high; $475.

F. Kroeber porcelain shelf clock with cobalt blue, gilt an floral decorated case, circa 1890, eight-day, time and strike, spring driven, 9" wide, 14" high; $675.

New Haven porcelain shelf clock with Van Dyke painting on case, 30-hour, time only, spring driven, 4" wide, 7" high; $175.

New Haven shelf clock with Jasperware case, 30-hour, time only, spring driven, 5-1/2" wide, 7" high; $175.

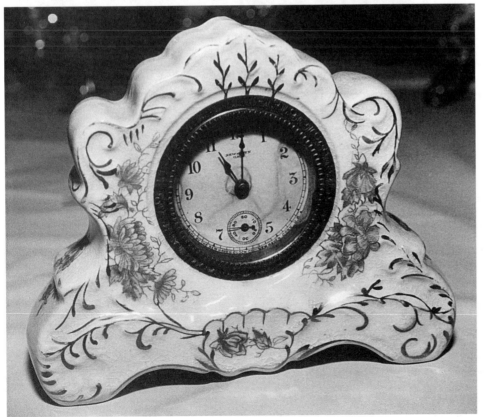

New Haven porcelain small case shelf clock, 30-hour time only, spring driven, 6" wide, 5" high; $75.

New Haven shelf clock (top row, from left) with Jasperware case, 30-hour, time only, spring driven, 4-1/2" high; $200. New Haven shelf clock with windmill painting on porcelain case, 30-hour, time only, spring driven, 4 1/2" wide, 9" high; $250. New Haven shelf clock (bottom row, from left) with Jasperware case, 30-hour, time only, spring driven, 4" wide, 5" high; $200. New Haven Delft porcelain shelf clock; 4-1/2" wide, 7" high; $250.

New Haven porcelain wall clock, one-day, time only, hair-spring driven, 7" wide, 8" high; 1-3/4" dial; $350.

New Haven "San Remo" porcelain wall clock, one-day, time only, hair-spring driven; 9" wide, 10" high; 2-1/2" dial; $375.

New Haven porcelain shelf clocks with blue and white delft colors, 7-1/2" to 10" high; $250 each.

New Haven porcelain hanging wall clock, patented July 1895, secondhand, eight-day, time only, 7" diameter; $300.

Unknown maker, shelf clock with Jasperware case, 30-hour, time only, spring driven, 4-1/2" wide, 6" high; $150.

Waterbury "Parlor Number 98" porcelain shelf clock, porcelain dial, eight-day, time and strike, nickel-plated movement, 9" wide, 11" high; $450.

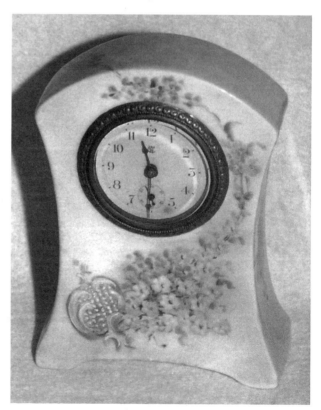

Waterbury porcelain shelf clock with floral design on case; 30-hour, time only, spring driven, 4" wide, 6" high; $175.

Ansonia "Arcadia" swing stature or figural clock, factory finished in bronze and nickel, originally made for jewelry store windows as attention getters, eight-day, time only, 4-1/2" dial, 3-1/2" high; $5,000.

Ansonia "Crystal Palace Number 1" with two figures under glass dome, mercury pendulum, time and strike, 15" wide, 19" high; $1,800.

Ansonia "Fantasy" statue clock, circa 1890, porcelain dial, open escapement, bronze finish, French rococo sash, eight-day, time and strike, 17-1/2" wide, 14" high; $750.

Ansonia "Fortuna" swing statue or figural clock, original bronze finish with gilt pendulum, eight-day, time, 4-1/2" dial, 30" high; $5,500.

Ansonia "Florida Group" statue clock of two girls with bird and flowers, open escapement, chartreuse dial, ormolu trimmings, eight-day, time and strike, 12" wide, 36" high; $4,750.

Ansonia "Juno" swing statue or figural clock, bronze finish, gilded pendulum, eight-day, time, 4-1/2" dial, 28" high; $3,800.

Ansonia "Lady with Peacock" black enameled base statue shelf clock with porcelain dial and open escapement, circa 1900, eight-day, time and strike, spring driven, 21" wide, 8-1/2" deep, 19-1/2" high; $850.

Ansonia "Pizarro" statue clock, original Japanese bronze finish, porcelain dial, visible escapement, beveled glass, rococo sash, eight-day, time and strike, 19-1/2" wide, 21-1/2" high; $1,600.

Ansonia "Olympia" statue clock, bronze finish, beveled glass, porcelain dial, balance wheel escapement, eight-day, time and strike, 15-1/2" wide, 24-1/2" high; $1,800.

Ansonia "Shakespeare" statue clock, porcelain dial, open escapement, bronze finish, French rococo sash, beveled glass, eight-day, time and strike, half hour gong, 17-1/2" wide, 15" high; $750.

Ansonia "Sibyl & Winter" statue clock with two cupids on base, original finish, eight-day, time and strike, 16-3/4" wide, 27" high; $2,900.

Ansonia "Summer and Winter" statue clock with a bronze finish, porcelain dial, open escapement, French rococo sash, beveled glass, eight-day, time and strike, with half hour gong, 24" wide, 22" high; $4,500.

Ansonia statue shelf clock with fisherman and hunter figures, double mercury style pendulum, 14" wide, 15" high; $700.

Ansonia black enameled statue shelf clock with bronzed metal decorations, porcelain shield dial numbers and open escapement, eight-day, time and strike, spring driven, 24" wide, 9" deep, 25" high; $1,500.

Ansonia black enameled metal statue shelf clock with gilded decorations, eight-day, time and strike, spring driven, 13-1/2" wide, 6" deep, 20" high; $550.

Ansonia novelty statue clock with croquet players, brass and porcelain dial, French rococo sash, patented April 28, 1876, time only, 8" wide, 7-1/2" high; $275.

W. L. Gilbert "Beatrice" with harp statue clock with bronze finish, mercury pendulum, open escapement, French rococo sash, eight-day, time and strike, 13" high; $1,250.

W. L. Gilbert "Mignon" statue clock, shown in their 1900 trade catalog, gilt finished case, statue and feet, porcelain dial, nickel-plate movement, marbleized base, all original, seven-day, time and strike; $575.

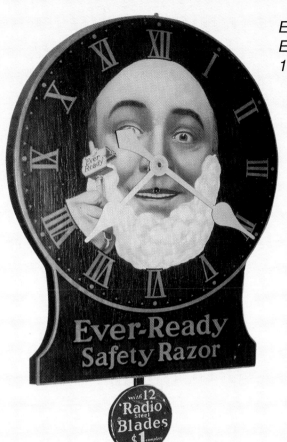

E. Ingraham wall clock advertising
Ever-Ready Safety Razor, time only,
18" diameter, 29" high; $4,000.

Coca-Cola electric wall clock, 16" wide,
16" high; $110.

Ansonia "La Cheze" Royal Bonn porcelain
shelf clock, eight-day, time and strike, 8"
wide, 10" high; $500.

Ansonia porcelain shelf clock with German case, eight-day, time and strike, 9½" wide, 9" high; $450.

New Haven "Thistle" porcelain hanging wall clock, with brass surround and wall chain, 15-day, time only, 10" wide, 14" high; $600.

Ansonia "Gloria" swing statue or figural clock, barbedienne bronze finish, gold numbers on dial and gilded pendulum, eight-day, time, 4½" wide, 28½" high; $5,500.

Ansonia "Rosalind" cast iron mantel clock with black enamel finish, porcelain dial, gilded decorations, seated lady on top, circa 1890, eight-day, time strike, 15" wide, 19" high; $650.

Ansonia "Hermes" statue clock, circa 1895, porcelain dial, eight-day, time and strike, 16" wide, 15" high. On the original clocks, the buyer had a choice of three different finishes: Japanese Bronze, Syrian Bronze or Barbedienne; $700.

Ansonia "Undine and Gloria" statue clock of girl with harp and wings. "Undine" is the name of the base and "Gloria" is the name of the statue. Porcelain dial, original finish, eight-day, time and strike, 16" wide, 28" high; $3,000.

Waterbury polished brass crystal regulator, mercury type pendulum, open escapement, time and strike, 7" wide, 9½" high; no price available.

Ansonia "Sovereign" polished mahogany crystal regulator, mercury pendulum, beveled glass, visible escapement, eight-day, half hour gong strike, 10½" wide, 18½" high; $3,600.

Curtis reproduction rosewood banjo wall clock, time only, weight driven, 10" wide, 42" high; $1,000.

Birge, Mallory and Company triple-decker shelf clock, circa 1845, brass strap movement invented by Joseph Ives, painted wood dial, original bottom glass tablet, eight-day, weight driven, 17" wide, 38" high; $700

Chauncey Jerome walnut veneer OG shelf clock, circa 1885, 30-hour, weight driven, 26" high; $350.

Manross Prichard & Co. mahogany OG shelf clock, circa 1850, 16" wide, 26½" high; $350.

Three alarms. Left, advertising clock for Muscatine, Iowa radio station KTNT; $50. Center, Big Ben eight-day alarm advertising Geo. H. Alps, Jeweler & House Furnisher, Burlington, Iowa; $65. Right, Chicken on dial advertising Cruso H.S. B. & Co.; $50.

New Haven Oak perpetual calendar shelf clock, with two parallel dials, inscribed lines, eight-day, time only, 14" wide, 13" high; $2,200.

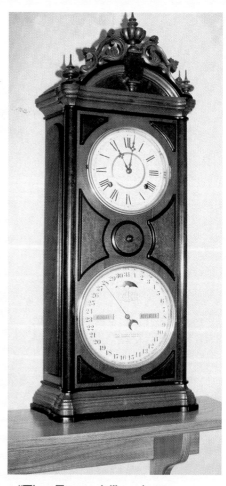

Ithaca Calendar Clock Company, "The Emerald" walnut perpetual calendar shelf clock with ebony trim. Provisions for the date, day and month are on the lower tablet, eight-day, time and strike, 14½" wide, 33" high; $3,400.

*Ithaca "Number 8 Shelf Library"
walnut perpetual calendar clock, with
burl inlay, 2" wide, 26½" high; $1,400.*

*American Clock Co. (address on label
is #3 Cortlandt, New Broadway) metal
mantel clock with mother-of-pearl inlay,
brass dial, eight-day, time and strike
(winders below dial), 8½" wide, 16" high;
$150*

*Seth Thomas metal front mantel clock,
nickel-plated over brass, minute hand,
time and alarm, 7" wide, 9" high; $150.*

Seth Thomas adamantine mottled marbleized finish mantel clock, eight-day, time and strike, 17" wide, 12" high; $300.

Waterbury cast iron black enameled mantel clock, brass dial, brass applied decorations, eight-day, time and strike, 9½" wide, 11" high; $275.

Sessions cast iron black enameled mantel clock, gilded decorations and feet, eight-day, time and strike, 15" wide, 10" high; $175.

8C

Ansonia "Triumph" oak shelf clock, circa 1890, mirror sides with brass cupid statues and other applied brass decorations, eight-day time and strike, 17" wide, 24½" high; $750.

E. Ingraham "Jasper" oak shelf clock, circa 1905, basket weave pressed designs and applied decorations, eight-day, time and strike, 15" wide, 23" high; $300.

E.O. Goodwin rosewood shelf clock, 1852-1855, with gold leaf stenciling on case, eight-day, time and strike, circa 1850s, 9½" wide, 15" high; $800.

W.L. Gilbert rosewood cottage shelf clock with octagon top, circa 1878-1885, at Winsted Connecticut, eight-day, time and strike, 10" wide, 13½" high; $175.

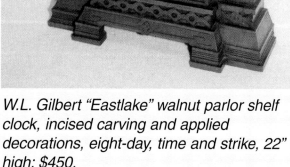

W.L. Gilbert "Eastlake" walnut parlor shelf clock, incised carving and applied decorations, eight-day, time and strike, 22" high; $450.

Waterbury rosewood Gothic steeple, shelf clock, circa 1870, 30-hour, time and strike, 19½" high; $225.

Ithaca Calendar Clock Company cast iron ionic perpetual calendar wall clock using H.B. Horton's calendar movement as seen on bottom dial, eight-day, time only, 9" wide, 19" high; $2,500.

Seth Thomas walnut octagonal wall clock with brass applied decorations, circa 1890, time only, 16" wide, 25" high; $375.

Seth Thomas rosewood pillar wall clock, prior to 1863 (Plymouth Hollow), original tablets, gilt columns, eight-day, weight driven, 16½' wide, 32" high; $550.

11C

Seth Thomas "Number 1 Extra" walnut regulator, circa 1875, secondhand, time only, weight driven, 13½" dial, 40" high; $2,500.

Waterbury oak regulator wall clock, circa 1912, secondhand, time only, weight driven, 37" high; $1,175.

E.N. Welch "Alexis Number 2" ebony decorated rosewood wall clock, circa 1875, applied gold leaf on tablet, eight-day, time only, 10" dial, 22" high; $400.

Ansonia "Baghdad" oak wall clock, incised carving and applied decorations, special Ansonia silver etched glass, time only, double weight driven, 16" wide, 50" high; $2,000.

Ken Williams walnut Jeweler's Regulator wall clock, 25 to 30 years old, eight-day, time only, 21" wide, 85" high; $3,000.

Seth Thomas "Regulator No. 7" walnut wall clock, circa 1885, hand carved cabinet, brass weight and pendulum, secondhand, Graham dead-beat escapement, eight-day, time only, 19" wide, 48" high; $10,000.

13C

Keebler cuckoo pendulette, molded wood, red and green foliage, 30-hour, time only, spring driven, 5" wide, 6½" high; $125.

American Clock Company metal case shelf clock, multi-colored with birds and flowers on case, 30-hour, time and strike, spring driven, 13" wide, 16" high; $400.

Parker Clock Company brass mantel clock with two cupids holding up the lamp post which have jeweled inserts, 30-hour, time only, 7" wide, 6 1/2" high; $1,200.

14C

New Haven fan novelty clock with brass stand and decorations, porcelain and brass dial, 30-hour, time only, 13" wide, 8" high; $850.

Ansonia metal bouncing doll, patent date on dial is Dec. 14, 1886, original German doll, 15½" high; $1,750.

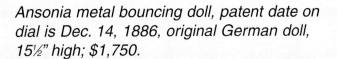

Lux Shmoo clock in its original box, never used; Li'l Abner and Daisy Mae are pictured on the box, 30-hour, time only, spring driven, 4" wide, 7" high; $550.

15C

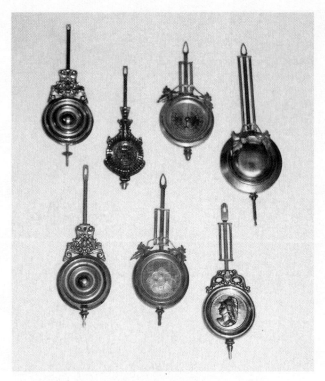

A miscellaneous collection of pendulums, no price available.

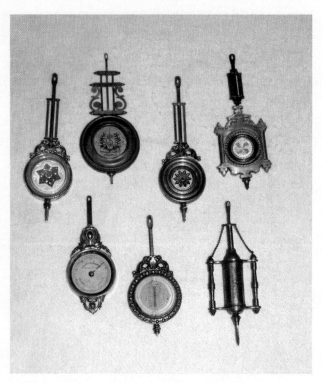

A miscellaneous collection of metal pendulums, no price available.

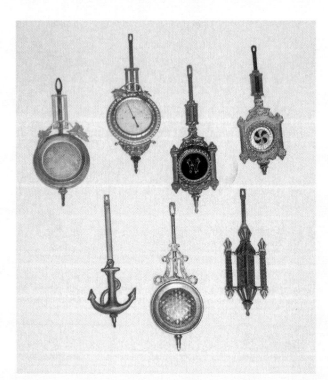

A miscellaneous collection of fancy pendulums, no price available.

A selection of indicator pendulums. From upper left clockwise: Gilbert, Waterbury, Ansonia American Clock Company, New Haven, Jarot's, Kroeber, and Jarot's in the center with hand missing; no price available.

W. L. Gilbert statue clock of a cupid stringing his bow, brass decorations and two cherubs at base, open escapement, porcelain dial, eight-day, time and strike, 10" wide, 33" high; $3,000.

W. L. Gilbert metal statue shelf clock with black enameled wooden base, eight-day, time and strike, spring driven 15" wide, 14-1/2" high; $400.

W. L. Gilbert statue clock, porcelain dial, metal and bronze clock and bronze figure at side with marbleized wooden base and cast feet, circa 1900, eight-day movement, 14-1/2" wide, 14" high; $500.

F. Kroeber walnut shelf clock with swinging child pendulum, eight-day, time and strike, spring driven, 12" wide, 20" high, 4-1/2" dial; $1,200. F. Kroeber statue shelf clock with embossed metal case and metal huntress figure on top, eight-day, time and strike, spring driven, 15" wide, 23" high, 4-1/2" dial; $550.

Label from F. Kroeber metal shelf clock with huntress figure.

F. Kroebee statue clock of a bowman on top of the metal clock which contains Kroeber's eight-day movement and a patented arrangement allowing the hands to be turned backwards without harm, eight-day, time and strike, 15" wide, 23" high; $950.

Label from F. Kroeber's statue clock reading, "This Clock contains F. Kroeber's Eight Day Movement with Polished Springs, Stop Work, and a Patented Arrangement allowing the hands to be turned backward, without injuring Striking Part. F. Kroeber, manufacturer and dealer in clocks."

F. Kroeber "Noiseless Rotary No. 2" statue clock of a woman with parasol sitting on top of a black enameled mantel clock. Patented June 18, 1878, when Kroeber was located at No. 14 Cortlandt Street (old Number 8) New York, eight-day, time and strike, 9-1/2" wide, 22" high; $1,500.

Label from F. Kroeber Eight Day Noiseless Rotary No. 2. Directions for Noiseless Rotary: "To regulate, for faster turn the ball itself to the right, for slower, to the left. Do not regulate by raising or lowering pendulum above. The point of pendulum ball must hang directly over the center of pointer."

New Haven statue clock of standing cupid figure, bronze and brass, 4-1/2" wide, 6-1/2" high; $150.

New Haven metal statue shelf clock with male child figure, 30-hour, time and strike, spring driven, 6" wide, 10" high; $200.

Metal statue shelf clock, marked "Sears, Roebuck & Co. Pat. Applied for" on back of case, 30-hour, time only, spring driven, 8" wide, 9-1/2" high; $110.

Seth Thomas & Sons "No. 8028" statue clock with work by Mitchell, Vance & Co. of a lady sitting on a throne playing a harp, circa 1880 to 1890, eight-day, time and strike, 14" wide, 18" high; $1,200.

Seth Thomas "The Whistler" gilt finished statue clock, eight-day, time, 14" high; $900.

Seth Thomas bronzed metal statue shelf clock with gilded decorations and porcelain dial, distributed by Mitchell Vance & Company, New York, 15-day, time and strike, spring driven, 14" wide, 18" high, 3" dial, no price available.

Unknown maker, Spanish American War iron front statue clock with bronze finish, time only, 10" wide, 11" high; $235.

Unknown maker, "Father Time" American brass finished statue clock, wall mounted, patented Sept. 22, 1885, time only, 10" wide, 11" high; $275.

Warner cupid iron front statue clock, dated May 15, 1906, porcelain face, bronze finish with cupid holding up the clock, time only, 6" wide, 9-1/2" high; $150.

Waterbury metal statue shelf clock with cupid playing the violin, circa 1890, 30-hour, time only, spring driven, 12" high; $200. Waterbury metal statue shelf clock with lady and child figures, patented 1896, 30-hour, time only, spring driven, 5-1/2" wide, 8" high; $200.

Waterbury and Canadian boudoir metal statue clocks, gilded finish, time only; left, Waterbury with buffalo, center, Canadian with child holding the clock, right, Waterbury, 5-1/2" to 9" high; $150 each.

Chapter 9

Shelf Clocks

In all probability the shelf clock became the first type of clock that fit easily into most homes. A table, shelf, or mantel was all that was needed to display this clock. Also, it could be produced more cheaply and easily than the bulkier tall case clocks. Before the introduction of shelf clocks, the clock maker and his apprentice or apprentices made clocks one at a time. Handcrafted methods required an inordinate amount of time to make a clock and consequently limited both the quantity and the production of clocks. When waterpower became more readily available to power machinery, it helped increase production.

When clocks were no longer made one at a time to fill individual orders, a new method of marketing was needed. Because retail stores could only sell small numbers of the manufactured clocks, clock makers often became itinerant merchants to sell their surplus supplies. Peddlers were also employed. In general, clock cases were not included because their omission reduced the cost to customers, as well as the weight the peddlers had to carry. Since all of the essential parts were there, customers could either hang up the clocks as they were or have cases custom made.

Four forms of shelf clocks took over the market during the last quarter of the 19th century. Walnut creations, used as parlor clocks, prevailed from around 1870 to 1900; "blacks" (black mantel clocks) were in favor from 1880 to just before 1920; oaks or kitchen clocks, mass produced by the millions, achieved their popularity from 1890 until well into the 1900s; and alarms were in vogue from 1875. These alarms were the earliest mechanical clocks and were used in monasteries by the monks to keep their appointments. These clocks were without dials and simply sounded a bell to awaken the monk.

Clock cases were made of wood with mahogany the chosen leader. However, clock makers were looking for other materials for the cases. Choices included iron cases, painted cases with Oriental designs, papier mâché with mother-of-pearl inlay and the early plastic celluloid, which was patented in 1869. It was not until the early 1900s, however, that these celluloid clocks appeared on the market. The majority of these were small, thirty-hour time only shelf clocks.

Two well-known varieties of alarm clock were manufactured by the Western Clock Company, which was established in La Salle, Illinois, in 1895. The "Big Ben" was marketed in 1910, and the "Little Ben" in 1915. Today these clocks are produced by Westclox, which became the company name in 1936.

A smaller form of the Connecticut shelf clock was the cottage clock, first made in the late 1800s. Most examples have 30-hour movements and wooden cases that are usually less than one foot in height with tops that were either flat or three-sided. Most were made in the last quarter or the 19th century.

A novel shelf clock that was developed by Ansonia Clock Company was the inkstand clock. It usually had two ink containers flanking the central clock with heights that ranged from 6 to 13 inches. They are usually one-day, time-only and may have a simple calendar attached. Two of Ansonia's clocks are named "Parlor Ink Stand No. 2" and "Office Ink Stand." Also producing inkstand clocks was Nicholas Muller's Sons. Several of their clocks have the option of a call bell on top of the clock. Oftentimes the inkbottles are cut glass.

A unique type of shelf clock appeared in the middle 1800s. It was made of papier mâché, which was mashed paper, mixed with glue and other adhesive materials, and could be easily molded. Decorations, such as mother-of-pearl and its imitations, were sometimes added to the finished product. Credited with being the largest producer of this type of clock was the Litchfield Manufacturing Co. of Litchfield, Connecticut. Also known to have produced these cases was the Otis & Upson Co. of Marion, Connecticut. After these clocks caught the public's attention, a substitute was introduced called "Iron Mâché," which was a painted and gilded process applied to cast iron fronts. The effect looked like genuine papier mâché.

The Jerome Company produced a large series of papier mâché shelf clocks. For their age they are reasonably inexpensive. Another unique manufactured clock was the pearl inlaid style that had model names like "Jenny Lind," "La Fayette," "Union," and "Washington." These names gave the clocks a patriotic feel.

Elias Ingraham of Bristol, Connecticut, is credited with designing the steeple clock with its pointed Gothic style. The clocks could have two or four steeples. They were produced around 1840 when brass-coiled springs were available. This was the time when clock makers developed an interest in the cheap brass movement clock. Steeple clocks are still made today. The heights of these clocks range from 10-1/2 inches to 24 inches with the two in-between sizes of 14-3/4 inches and 20 inches. The smallest steeples have been called sub miniatures.

When Elisah C. Brewster and Elias and Andrew Ingrahams were in partnership in the early 1800s, one of their advertisements read as follows: "Have constantly on hand, at their factory in Bristol, Conn. Their various styles of patent spring eight-day and thirty-hour brass clocks, in mahogany, zebra, rosewood and black walnut cases."

Connecticut shelf clocks were popular commodities from the late 1840s until the early 1900s. One of these clocks, the beehive, which has a rounded Gothic arch, resembled the inverted hull of a ship. Its average size was 11 inches wide and 18-1/2 inches high. Most clock makers produced this popular clock.

Decorating clock tablets was an easy task in the 19th century because hundreds of different stencil patterns were available. By the late 1800s, clock tablets with decalcomania (decals) transfers could be easily purchased. These patterns were not as desirable, however, as the reversed painted ones. Etched glass examples appeared after 1840, but most were used on better clocks.

In the late 1800s, the Ansonia Clock Company offered a group of three oak shelf clocks for a marked down price of $12.60. They were eight-day clocks named, "Gallatin," "Echo," and "Griswold." Ansonia claimed that these gong strike clocks would be sure sellers and big money makers.

Seth Thomas, in an attempt to outdo the other clock companies, produced a series of "City" clocks that were named after American and International cities. The clocks were all eight-day time and strike, spring driven, and available in walnut, rosewood, or oak cases. Four of the international cities in this series were Athens, Cambridge, Oxford, and Rome. United States cities used in this series were Atlanta, Boston, Buffalo, Detroit, Newark, New York, Omaha, Peoria, Pittsburgh, Santa Fe, St. Paul, Tacoma, and Topeka.

In the 1880s, the New Haven Clock Company developed its clock series in which the mantel, eight-day time and strike clocks with walnut cases were named after world rivers. Some names selected were Rhine, Thames, Seine, Volga, Tiber, and Danube.

Not to be outdone, the W. L. Gilbert Clock Company joined what seemed to be the series clock competition. It came out with a series of fish and animal clocks around 1891. These clocks had eight-day movements and were finished in either oak or walnut. The cases were named after six fish bass, carp, pike, salmon, shark, and trout and were all about 22 inches in height. The animal cases featuring the buffalo, hyena, leopard, lion, panther, and tiger were around 21 inches high.

The Welch, Spring and Company developed a series of clocks that were named after artists from the opera and theater. One of the stars whose name was used in its clock styles and movements was Adelina Patti, an opera prima donna.

Some of these series clocks had historical figures such as Admiral Dewey (produced by Ingraham and Welch), President McKinley (produced by Ingraham), and Admiral Schley (produced by Welch) on the middle top front of the cases. Clock labels, generally 10 by 12 inches in dimension, were customarily placed on the inside back board of the cases. In the center of the label the type of clock, the maker and his location were found. Almost always included on the label was the phrase, "Warranted if Well Used."

The larger clock companies produced the oak or kitchen clocks in large numbers, with Ingraham ranking as the highest producer. Heights were about 23 inches with substantial eight-day longwearing striking movements. The pressed design on many of the oak shelf clocks was created by a rotary press that forced the design into the wood that had been previously softened with steam. They featured a glass panel as the tablet, decorated in bronze or silver gilt. Their $4 or $6 price tag enabled many American homes to display one of these clocks that remained popular from the late 1800s to around 1915. During this time, millions of these inexpensive clocks were manufactured.

Mantel clock assortments were also offered at reasonable prices. A special carload buy of six highly embossed oak cases with E. Ingraham movements was listed at $8.20.

An advertisement read, "Our imitation French marble clocks are a reproduction of the French designs in wood, HIGHLY POLISHED, nicely engraved and gilded. We guarantee the finish on these cases to stand equal to any iron case on the market."

Another sales promotion by Ansonia presented an exciting offer in its 1893 clock special. The ad encouraged buyers by saying, "Our New Bankers Clock Assortment with all six clocks available for $12.50." The names of the three with walnut cases were "Berkley," "Buffalo," and "Beaver." The three oak clocks listed were "Belmont," "Bedford," and "Burton." All of these clocks were eight-day strike clocks, 22-1/2 inches high with 6-inch dials. The two that had alarms were the walnut "Beaver" and the oak "Burton." The shipping case was provided, but the customer had to take all six clocks.

Because of the shortage of black walnut, which had been used extensively for clock cases, marbleized or black mantel clocks became popular around 1880. Their black marble top finish was kept clean with the use of sweet oil. Its use for this purpose was suggested in an early century Sears, Roebuck Catalogue. Many of these clocks were elaborately engraved and inlaid to emulate black marble and onyx mantel clocks. Added brass ornamentation gave them character. In addition, the use of enameled cast iron gave them a black marble look. These mantel clocks were called "Blacks." The materials used in the production of these blacks were marble, black iron, and black enameled wood.

In company with the mantel clocks were the tambour clocks, which had rounded tops and were often called "camelbacks" or "hunchbacks." This style was introduced at the beginning of the 20th century and is still being produced today.

A finish used exclusively by Seth Thomas on mantel and tambour clocks was called the adamantine finish. This finish, extremely hard and everlasting, was an exact copy of the French patterns in marble and onyx. This gave wooden clocks a marble look, finely polished and finished in a perfect imitation of marble. Major clock catalogs featured the black enamel wood clocks and described them as "Finished to imitate Italian marble and green Mexican onyx." In a trade catalog by E. Ingraham Co. it was stated, "Our imitation French marble clocks are a reproduction of the French designs in wood, HIGHLY POLISHED, nicely engraved and gilded. We guarantee the finish of these cases to stand equal to any iron case on the market."

Missing clock parts can be readily acquired today from companies that produce hands, dials, finials, and other small clock parts. If parts are replaced, it is advisable to keep the originals. Also available are bronze statues that were top pieces for clocks and can take the place of damaged or missing ones. Some collectors do not make changes, but keep their clocks in as near their original condition as possible.

Is there any easy way to remember that raising the bob on the pendulum rod shortens the pendulum's swing so that the clock goes faster, and lowering it slows down the clock's speed? A four word catch phrase that we have heard is, "Lower Slower-Higher Sprier".

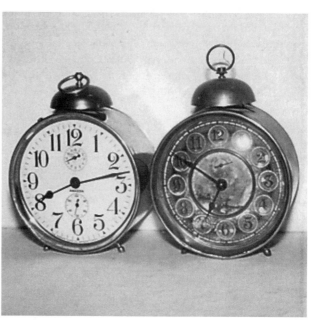

Ansonia "Snap" alarm clock with dog beneath clock, 8-3/4" high; $400, Ansonia "Pride" alarm clock circa 1880, with figures flanking clock, 7-1/2" high; $425.

Ansonia "Amazon" alarm clock, 5" dial; $150. Ansonia alarm clock, 5" dial; $150.

Darche Manufacturing Company, Chicago, metal bank (marked "Fireproof, Safety Deposit") shelf clock, patented July 12, 1910, 30-hour, time and alarm, 13" wide, 6" deep, 8" high; $125.

E. Ingraham "Victory" alarm clock, early 1900; $35

Echo, patented March 27, 1877, hand of figure moves automatically and rings bell, 7-1/2" high; $2,250.

National Call, eight-day, time and alarm, radium dial that glows in the dark; $85.

New Haven "intermittent" alarm clock; $70.

New Haven "Beacon" alarm clock in original box,
4-1/2" wide, 6" high; $125.

New Haven Giant alarm clock, 5" dial; $150.

Parker Clock Co. alarm clock with brass statue of a girl carrying a basket, 30 hour, time and alarm, 7" wide, 13" high; $900.

"Radium" alarm clock (from left), patented December 31, 1912; $40. W.L. Gilbert alarm clock, patented February 16, 1904; $40. Ansonia "Simplex Automatic" alarm clock, patented November 14, 1914; $40. The National Call alarm clock with luminous dial and hands; $40.

Seth Thomas iron case shelf clock with brass face, dated January 25, 1898, eight-day, time, strike, and alarm, spring driven, 8-1/2" wide, 10" high; $125.

Unknown maker, wooden castle shelf clock, 30-hour time and alarm, spring driven, 7-1/2" wide, 13" high; $175.

Unknown maker, advertising for "Quincy" on dial, patented 1907, dual alarm; $65.

Unknown maker, grandfather's moon dial, time and alarm, 6" high; $1,500.

Unknown maker, advertising Paul's Jewelry Co., Burlington, Iowa, time and alarm; $75.

Unknown maker, advertising Jordan Jeweler & Optician, Davenport, Iowa on dial; $75.

Unknown maker novelty alarm clock with Amos & Andy
with Kingfish on dial, 5" diameter; $50.

Unknown maker, double bell Snoopy alarm clock, 3-1/2"
diameter; $25.

Unknown maker, alarm clock with advertising for McCabe Jewelers, Rock Island, Illinois on dial; $70.
Unknown maker alarm clock with advertising for Frank the Jeweler, Muscatine, Iowa dial; $60.

Westclox "Ironclad" metal shelf clock (left to right), 30-hour, time and alarm, spring driven, 4-1/4" wide, 5-1/4" high; $35. USN NM metal shelf clock, 30-hour, time and alarm, 2-3/4" high; $35. Ansonia "The Plato" metal digital shelf clock, patented July 7, 1908, 30-hour, time only, 4-1/2" high; $250. Ansonia "Square Rascal" metal shelf clock, 30-hour, time and alarm, 2-1/4" wide, 2-3/4" high; $35.

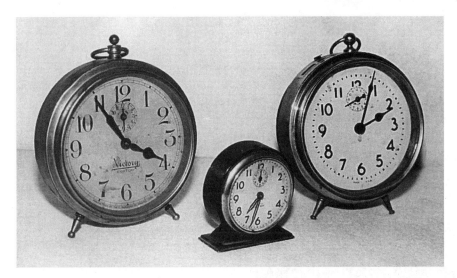

Westclox "Baby Ben" alarm clock (left to right), patented 1932; $35 Westclox "Big Ben" alarm clock, dated March 1, 1922; $35. Westclox "Baby Ben" alarm clock, patented November 9, 1920; $35.

Westclox Big Ben with advertising for C.G. Samuelson Jeweler, Orion, Illinois on dial; $75.

Ansonia "Boston Extra" cast-iron black enameled mantel clock, circa 1890, porcelain dial, open escapement, green pillars, eight-day, time and strike, 15" wide, 11-1/2" high; $350.

Ansonia "Belgium" cast-iron, black enameled mantel clock, circa 1890, porcelain dial, dragons on each end, eight-day, time and strike, 18" wide, 12" high; $400.

Ansonia "Capri" cast-iron, black enameled mantel clock, circa 1890, porcelain dial, open escapement, eight-day, time and strike, 15" wide, 12" high; $350.

Ansonia "Carlisle" cast-iron, black enameled mantel clock, circa 1901, gilded pillars, lion heads and feet, eight-day, time and strike, 17" wide, 10" high; $200.

Ansonia "Denmark" cast-iron, black enameled mantel clock, circa 1890, gold tinted face, three marbleized columns on each side, eight-day, time and strike, 16-1/2" wide, 12" high; $500.

Ansonia "La France" cast-iron, black enameled mantel clock, circa 1890, brass sunburst dial, gilded decorations, eight-day, time and strike, 11-1/2" wide, 11" high; $200.

Ansonia "Lisle" cast-iron, black enameled mantel clock, gilt-applied decorations, circa 1890, eight-day, time and strike, 11" wide, 10-1/2" high; $300.

Ansonia "London Extra" cast-iron, black enameled mantel clock, circa 1895, brass sunburst dial, gilded pillar and lion heads, eight-day, time and strike, 11-1/2" wide, 12-1/2" high; $300.

Ansonia "Montague" cast-iron, black enameled mantel clock, circa 1890, porcelain face, gilded decorations, eight-day, time and strike, 13" wide, 12" high; $300.

Ansonia "Unique" black enameled metal case mantel clock, circa 1890, slate dial, gilded decorations, eight-day, time and strike, 9-1/2" wide, 10" high; $250.

Label on back of Ansonia mantel clock. Unusual to have label on this type of clock. It reads, "Prize medal awarded Paris Exposition, 1878..."

Ansonia cast-iron, black enameled mantel clock, circa 1890, porcelain dial, open escapement, applied gilded decorations, eight-day, time and strike, 13" wide, 10" high; $350.

Ansonia cast-iron, black enameled mantel clock, slate dial, open escapement, four marbleized columns and trim, circa 1890, eight-day, time and strike, 16" wide, 13" high; $500.

Ansonia plush mantel clock, circa 1895, flush dial, beveled glass, gilded winged dragon feet and lion heads, eight-day, time and strike, 10-1/2" wide, 12-3/4" high; $300.

Ansonia black enameled metal case mantel clock with gilded decorations, eight-day, time and strike, spring driven, 12" wide, 10-1/2" high; $125.

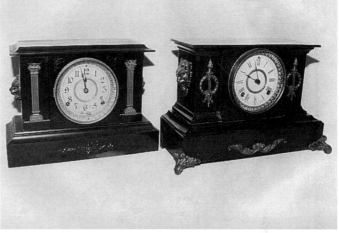

Ansonia black enameled metal case mantel clock with gilded decorations, eight-day, time and strike, spring driven, 14" wide, 10" high; $125. Ansonia black enameled metal case mantel clock with gilded decorations, eight-day, time and strike, spring driven, 16-1/2" wide, 10-1/2" high; $125.

Ansonia black enameled metal case mantel clock with open escapement, eight-day, time and strike, spring driven, 9-1/2" wide, 10-1/2" high; $275.

W. L. Gilbert "Curfew" Italian marble finish mantel clock, circa 1910, eight day, time and strike, 16" wide, 17-1/2" high; $375.

E. Ingraham black enameled wooden case mantel clock with marbleized trim and gilded decorations, eight-day, time and strike, spring driven, 18" wide, 11-1/2" high; $125.

F. Kroeber black enameled metal mantel clock with porcelain dial, eight-day, time and strike, spring driven, 13" wide, 12" high; $250.

New Haven black enameled metal case mantel clock with open escapement, eight-day, time and strike, spring driven, 14-1/2" wide, 10" high; $175.

Sessions cast-iron, black enameled mantel clock, gilded pillars, lion heads and feet, 15-1/2" wide, 10-1/2" high; $225.

New Haven black enameled metal case mantel clock with applied gilded decorations, eight-day, time and strike, spring driven, 10" wide, 11" high; $295.

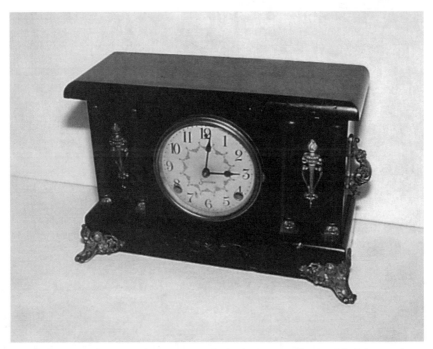

Sessions cast-iron, black enameled mantel clock, green pillars, gilded decorations and feet, eight-day, time and strike, 15" wide, 10" high; $165.

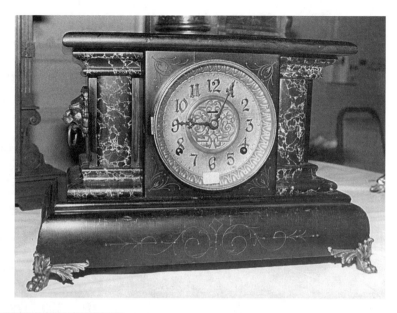

Sessions black enameled wooden case mantel clock with marbleized trim and brass dial, circa 1910-20, eight-day, time and strike, spring driven, 17" wide, 11" high; $125.

Sessions black enameled wooden case mantel clock with marbleized trim and gilded decorations, eight-day, time and strike, spring driven, 15" wide, 10-1/2" high; $125.

Seth Thomas adamantine black enameled mantel clock, circa 1895, with four columns, gilded decorations and marbleized ends, eight-day, time and strike, 18" wide, 12" high; $325.

Seth Thomas adamantine black enameled mantel clock, four marbleized columns, copper wash finish, eight-day, time and strike, 17-1/2" wide, 12" high; $300.

Seth Thomas "Arno" adamantine black enameled mantel clock with gilded and marbleized columns, eight-day, time and strike, 12" wide, 11-1/2" high; $270.

Seth Thomas wooden case, adamantine mantel clock to resemble ebony with marbleized trim, patented September 7, 1880, eight-day, time and strike, spring driven, 11-1/2" wide, 11" high; $125. E. Ingraham mantel clock with black enameled case to resemble ebony, marbleized columns, brass and porcelain dial, eight-day, time and strike, spring driven, 16-1/2" wide, 11" high; $125.

Seth Thomas black enameled adamantine finish mantel clock, brass dial, feet and lion heads at each end, dated Sept. 7, 1880, 17" wide, 11-1/2" high; $225.

Unknown maker, black enameled metal case mantel clock with marbleized edging, eight-day, time only, spring driven, 8-1/2" wide, 10-1/2" high; $275.

Waterbury cast iron black enameled mantel clock, porcelain and brass dial, brass applied decorations, eight-day, time and strike, 10" wide, 11" high; $300.

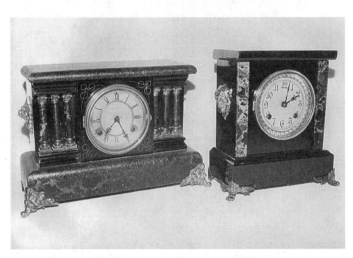

Waterbury artificially grained wooden mantel clock with marbleized columns and gilded decorations, eight-day, time and strike, spring driven, 16" wide, 10-1/2" high; $125. New Haven black enameled wooden mantel clock with marbleized edging and gilded decorations, eight-day, time and strike, spring driven, 11" wide, 12" high; $125.

Waterbury iron front black shelf clock with floral and gilded decorations, circa 1850, 30-hour, time and strike, spring driven, 12" wide, 16" high, 3-1/2" dial; $200.

E.N. Welch "Albani" marble mantel clock, porcelain dial, open escapement, beveled glass, eight-day, time and strike (contains the famous Patti movement), 14-1/2" wide, 10" high; $600.

Ansonia "Cabinet Antique" polished mahogany cabinet clock with antique brass trimmings, French sash, finials, porcelain and brass face, eight-day, time and strike, 9-1/4" wide, 20" high; $2,750.

Ansonia "The Senator" polished mahogany cabinet clock, antique brass trimmings, silver dial, eight-day, time and half hour gong strike, 19" wide, 22" high; $4,000.

Ansonia "Cabinet Antique Number 1" polished mahogany shelf clock, circa 1896, antique brass trimmings, porcelain and brass dial, eight-day, time and half hour, Old English bell strike, 11-1/2" wide, 18-3/4" high; $3,750.

Ansonia "Lily" inkwell calendar clock (left), 30-hour, 7" high; $1,200. Ansonia "Gem" inkwell perpetual calendar clock, 7-1/2" high; $1,400.

Ansonia simple calendar shelf clock, eight-day, 8-1/2" high; $300.

W.L. Gilbert "Elberon" oak simple calendar shelf clock with McCabe's November 10, 1896 patent calendar movement, repainted tablet has flowers instead of birds, this clock was sold by the Southern Calendar Clock Company in the late 1890s, eight-day, time and strike, spring driven, 15" wide, 30-1/2" high, 8" dial; $1,700.

W.L. Gilbert rosewood simple calendar clock with G.B. Owen's April 24. 1886 patent calendar movement, eight-day, time and strike, spring driven. 10" wide, 13" high, 5" dial; $1,000.

W. L. Gilbert walnut simple calendar shelf clock with moon phase, eight-day. time and strike, spring driven, 11-1/2" wide, 19" high, 5" dial; $1,000.

Ithaca Calendar Clock Company walnut "Index" with two patent dates—April 18, 1865 and Aug. 28, 1866, perpetual calendar shelf clock manufactured for Lynch Brothers with provisions for the date, day and month on the lower round tablet, eight-day, time and strike, 17" wide, 33" high; $3,400.

Ithaca Calendar Clock Company, "Farmers" walnut per-petual calendar shelf clock, circa 1865, with Welch move-ment and provisions for the date, day, and month on the lower tablet, eight-day, time and strike, 25-1/2" high; $700.

Ithaca Calendar Clock Company walnut perpetual cal-endar shelf clock with ebony applied decorations and turned columns. The dates of the month are in gold around the outer rim of the bottom tablet, and the days and months are on rotating tubes behind the tablet, eight-day, time and strike, 10" wide, 20" high; $4,200.

Ithaca walnut double-dial calendar shelf clock (left) with H.B. Horton's August 28. 1866 patent calendar movement, eight-day, time and strike, spring driven. 12" wide, 25" high, 5-1/2" upper dial, 7" lower dial; $900. Ithaca walnut double-dial calendar shelf clock with H.B. Horton's August 28, 1866 patented calen-dar movement, an exact copy of case and dials but with original movement, eight-day, time and strike, spring driven, 10" wide, 20" high, 5" upper dial, 7" lower dial; $1,500 for exact copy, $2,500 for original clock.

F. Kroeber oak "Summit" centrifugal calendar clock, circa 1877, eight-day, time and strike, 21-1/2" high; $600.

Ithaca Calendar Clock Company walnut perpetual calendar shelf clock with ebony applied decorations and turned columns. The dates are in silver around the outer rim of the bottom tablet, and the two rectangular windows show the day and month, eight-day, time and strike, 10" wide, 28" high; $3,200.

Close-up of F. Kroeber's calendar shelf clock dial which has dates encircling inner rim and "Calendar Patented July 1877" at the top of the inner circle.

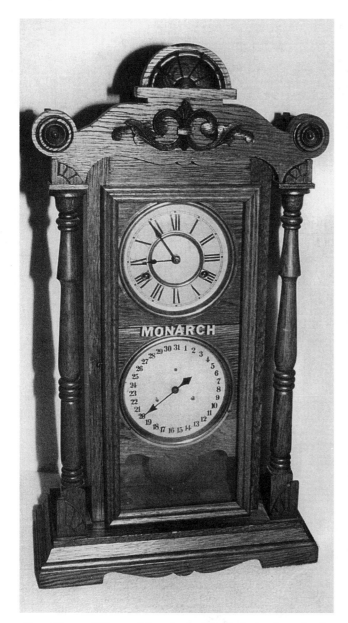

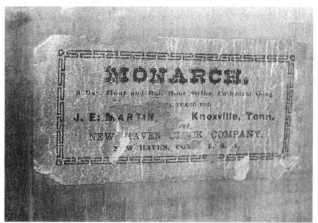

Close-up of label from New Haven double-dial simple calendar shelf clock.

New Haven "Monarch" oak double-dial simple calendar clock, eight-day, time and strike, spring driven, 15" wide, 27" high, 5" dial; $1,000.

New Haven oak simple calendar shelf clock, circa 1885, eight-day, time and strike, spring driven, 15" wide, 25" high; $300.

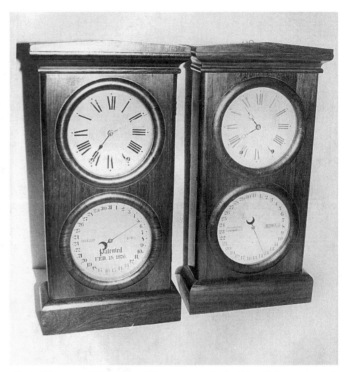

Seth Thomas "Number 3" rosewood double-dial perpetual calendar shelf clocks, left clock patented February 15, 1876, right clock patented January 31, 1860, eight-day, time and strike, spring driven, 13-1/2" wide, 27" high, 7-1/2" dials; $800 each.

The "Ridgeway," a 25-year-old walnut reproduction calendar shelf clock, eight-day, time and strike, 15-1/2" wide, 27" high; $300.

Seth Thomas "Number 5" walnut double-dial calendar clock with R.T. Andrew's February 15, 1876, patent calendar movement, eight-day, time and strike, spring driven, 12-1/2" wide, 20" high, 7" dials; $950.

Seth Thomas "Calendar Number 10" walnut double-dial calendar shelf clock with R.T. Andrew's February 15, 1876, patent calendar movement, eight-day, time and strike, weight driven, 22" wide, 36-1/2" high; 9-1/2" dials; no price available.

Seth Thomas walnut double-dial calendar clock, circa 1876, eight-day, time and strike, spring driven, 16" wide, 32" high, 8" dial; $1,750.

Unknown maker, mahogany simple calendar shelf clock, time only, eight-day, pendulum movement, 10" wide, 17" high; $700.

Waterbury "Buffalo" walnut simple calendar clock (left), late 1800s, eight-day, time and strike, spring driven, 17-1/2" wide, 27" high 7" dial; $600. Waterbury "Number 38 Calendar" walnut double-dial perpetual calendar clock, eight-day, time only, spring driven, 13-1/2" wide, 26" high, 5" dials, $800.

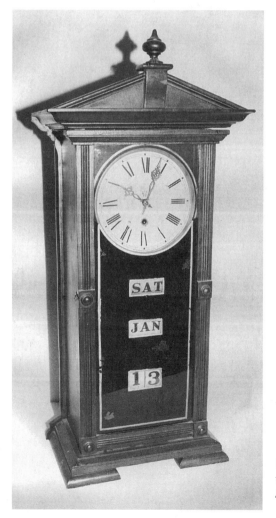

Waterbury "Oswego" oak double-dial perpetual calendar clock (left), with A.F. Well's July 30, 1889, patent calendar movement, eight-day, time and strike, spring driven, 17" wide, 28" high, 7" dial; $800. Waterbury "Number 43 Calendar" oak double dial perpetual calendar shelf clock, A.F. Well's July 30, 1889 patent calendar movement, eight-day, time and strike, spring driven, 16" wide, 29" high, 7" dials; $800.

Waterbury walnut simple calendar shelf clock, circa 1890, with roller type calendar movement, eight-day, time only, spring driven, 13-1/2" wide, 32" high, 7" dial; $2,500.

Close-up of roller type calendar movement on Waterbury simple calendar shelf clock.

Waterbury mahogany veneered calendar clock with Seem's dial, patent January 7, 1868, eight-day, time and strike, spring driven, 11" wide, 16-1/2" high; $700.

E.N. Welch "Italian" round top double-dial perpetual calendar shelf clock, eight-day, time and strike, spring driven, 12" wide, 20" high, 6-1/2" dial; $650.

E.N. Welch walnut perpetual calendar clock with Franklin-Morse's June 12, 1883, patent calendar movement, eight-day, time and strike, spring driven, 16" wide, 22-1/2" high, 5" dial; $900. Waterbury walnut double-dial perpetual calendar clock with S.W. Feishtinger's October 9, 1894, patent calendar movement, eight-day, time and strike, spring driven, 13" wide, 22" high, 5" dial; $650.

E.N. Welch walnut double-dial perpetual calendar clock, circa 1889, exact copy of case with original works, eight-day, time and strike, spring driven, 20" wide, 31-1/2" high, 7" dials; $1,500 for copy, $2,200 for original.

E.N. Welch "Arditi" walnut double-dial perpetual calendar shelf clock with D.J. Gale's April 21, 1885 patent calendar movement, eight-day, time and strike, spring driven, 17-1/2" wide, 27-1/2" high, 7" dials; $1,800.

Boston Clock Company carriage clock, brass frame and carrying handle, 3-1/2" wide, 5" high; $350-$450.

Boston Clock Company carriage clock, patented Dec. 20, 1880, brass case, porcelain dial, tandem wind spring movement, 30-hour, time only, 4" wide, 6-1/2" high; $3,750.

F. Kroeber carriage clock, circa 1889, brass case, glass sides and time only, 8" high; $200.

Waterbury repeater carriage clock, brass frame and carrying handle, 3-1/2" wide, 4" high; $350-$450.

New Haven "Acme" brass clock with top handle, 30-hour, time only; $350.

Waterbury "Hornet" brass clock with ivory dial, glass cylinder, circa 1900, 30-hour, time only, 2-3/4" diameter; $225.

New Haven tusculor case (celluloid) shelf clock, dated December 23, 1918, on base, 30-hour, time only, spring driven, 4" wide, 3-1/2" high; $55.

New Haven celluloid shelf clock, 30-hour, time only, spring driven, 5-1/2" wide, 4" high; $75. New Haven "Junior Tattoo Movement" shelf clock, patented April 7, 1904, 30-hour, time and alarm, spring driven, 3" diameter; $45.

Seth Thomas miniature celluloid case mantel clock, 30-hour, time only, spring driven, 6-1/4" wide, 4-1/4" high; $35.

Unknown maker, celluloid shelf clock, 30-hour, time only, spring driven, 4" wide 4 -1/2"high; $55. Unknown maker, green celluloid shelf clock, with pearl and rhinestone jeweled case, 6-1/2" wide, 3-1/2" high; $85.

Waterbury celluloid shelf clock, 30-hour, time only, spring driven, 5" wide, 4-1/4" high; $55.

Ansonia Brass & Copper Company mahogany veneered steeple clock, circa 1854-1879, eight-day, time, strike, and alarm, spring driven, 11" wide, 20" high, 4-1/2" dial; $300.

Brewster & Ingraham mahogany ribbed Gothic shelf clock, original brass springs replaced, eight-day, time and strike, 10-1/2" wide, 19" high; $450.

Brewster & Ingraham burled walnut Gothic shelf clock, brass springs. replaced tablet and hands, eight-day, time and strike, 10-1/2" wide, 19" high; $400.

J.C. Brown rosewood ribbed front Gothic shelf clock, circa 1855, time and strike, 10-1/2" wide, 19" high; $1,200.

J.C. Brown rosewood Gothic shelf clock, circa 1855, dial reads: "J.C. Brown, Forestville Company," replaced tablet, eight-day, time and strike, 10-1/2" wide, 19" high; $400.

J.C. Brown & Company rosewood ripple front steeple shelf clock, circa 1855, time and strike, 10" wide, 20" high; $1,650.

Burroughs Clock Company cherry miniature rounded steeple or onion top clock, circa 1870-1874, 5" wide, 7" high; $125.

W.L. Gilbert rosewood steeple clock, 30-hour, time and strike, spring driven, 11" wide, 20" high; $150.

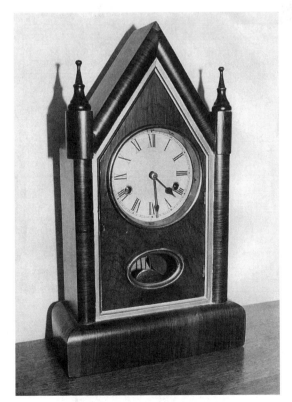

W.L. Gilbert mahogany veneered steeple clock, circa 1870, 30-hour, time and strike, spring driven; $165.

Elisha Manross rosewood steeple shelf clock, 30-hour, time and strike, 10" wide, 20" high; $250.

W.L. Gilbert mahogany veneered steeple clock, eight-day, time and strike, spring driven, 1/4" wide, 16" high; $150.

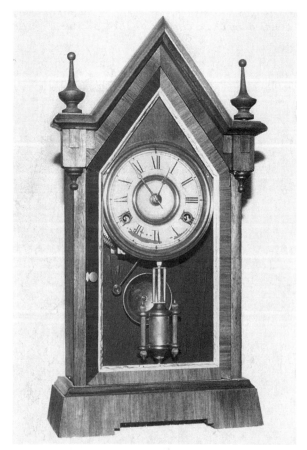

New Haven "Jerome" rosewood steeple clock, eight-day, time and strike, spring driven, 10" wide, 19" high; 4-1/2" dial; $150.

New Haven oak steeple clock, eight-day, time and strike, spring driven, 9-1/2" wide, 15-1/2" high; $175.

Seth Thomas "Prospect Number 1" mahogany Gothic shelf clock, circa 1910, time and strike, 13-1/2" high; $220.

Seth Thomas mahogany beehive shelf clock, eight-day, time and Westminster chimes, spring driven, 10" wide, 15" high; $690.

Tiffany battery operated mahogany Gothic shelf clock, circa 1895, beveled glass, time only, 10" wide, 16" high; $1,250.

E.N. Welch "Beehive Model" rosewood shelf clock, eight-day, time and strike, spring driven, 10-1/2" wide, 19" high, 6" dial; $350.

E.N. Welch mahogany steeple shelf clock, time, strike and alarm, 10" wide, 19-1/2" high; $300.

E. Ingraham "Admiral Dewey" pressed oak shelf clock, circa 1899-1905, eight-day, time, strike and alarm, spring driven, 15" wide, 23" high, 5" dial;, $500; E. Ingraham "President McKinley" pressed oak shelf clock, circa 1899-1905, eight-day, time and strike, spring driven, 15" wide, 23" high, 5" dial; $500.

E. Ingraham "F.D.R. The Man of the Hour" metal electric shelf clock, circa 1940, 9" wide, 14" high; $95.

E. Ingraham pressed oak simple calendar shelf clock from the River Series with a ship on the tablet, circa 1905, eight-day, time and strike, spring driven, 15" wide, 23" high, 5" dial; $500. E. Ingraham "Liberty" walnut shelf clock, eight-day, time, strike, and alarm, spring driven, 14-1/2" wide, 23" high, 5" dial; $500.

E.N. Welch "Admiral Schley" pressed oak shelf clock (left) with the ship "Olympia" on the tablet, circa 1900, eight-day, time and strike, spring driven, 15-1/2" wide, 24" high, 5" dial; $500. Seth Thomas "Fleet Number 2" oak shelf clock with Teddy Roosevelt's four battleships that he sent around the world on a peace cruise pictured on the tablet, eight-day, time and strike, spring driven 15" wide, 24" high, 5" dial; $500.

Waterbury "Admiral Dewey" metal shelf clock, 8" wide, 10" high; $195.

Label from Seth Thomas "Fleet Number 2" oak shelf

Close-up of four battleships pictured on the tablet of Seth Thomas "Fleet Number 2" oak shelf clock.

Ansonia "Lydia" cast-iron mantel clock, open escapement, with cherubs on top of clock, eight-day, time and strike, with matching pair of urns, 19-1/2" high; $3,000.

Ansonia "The Virginia" cast-iron mantel clock with statue, "Opera" on top of clock, open escapement, brass and silver dial, silver panels on each side of clock, eight-day, time and strike, with matching pair of urns, 21" wide, 25" high; $4,500.

Cast metal ornament for use on flat top clock. Many similar ornaments were available from Ansonia Clock Company, 9" wide, 6" high; $75.

W.L. Gilbert oak tambour mantel clock, circa 1880, time and strike, 9-1/2" high; $110.

W.L. Gilbert mantel clock with artificially grained wooden case and brass bell on top that rings every half hour, circa 1880, eight-day, time and strike, spring driven, 17" wide, 17-1/2" high; $375.

E. Ingraham miniature (baby camel back) wooden tambour mantel clock, metal dial, 8-1/2" wide, 5-1/2" high; $85.

E. Ingraham oak mantel clock, circa 1895, time and strike, 10" high; $120.

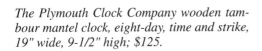

The Plymouth Clock Company wooden tambour mantel clock, eight-day, time and strike, 19" wide, 9-1/2" high; $125.

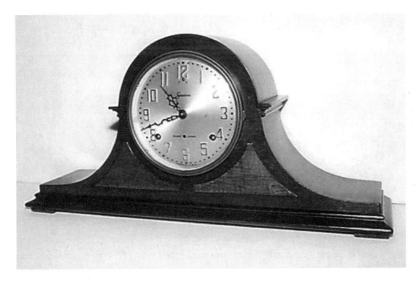

Sessions mahogany tambour mantel clock, eight-day, time and strike. Westminster chimes, patented 1929, 18" wide, 17-1/2" high; $175.

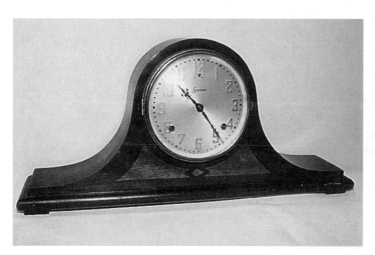

Sessions "Dulciana" mahogany tambour mantel clock, eight-day, time and strike, 21-1/2" wide, 10" high; $175.

Label on the back of the Sessions "Dulciana" mantel clock.

Sessions mahogany round top shelf clock, circa 1930, eight-day, time and strike, spring driven, 9" wide, 11" high; $95.

Sessions Clock Co. cherry stained mantel clock, circa 1910, six columns, gilded feet and lion heads, eight-day, time and strike, 14-1/2" wide, 10-1/2" high; $175.

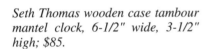

Seth Thomas wooden case tambour mantel clock, 6-1/2" wide, 3-1/2" high; $85.

Seth Thomas adamantine (rosewood finish) tambour mantel clock, eight-day, time and strike, 17-1/2" wide, 10-1/2" high; $245.

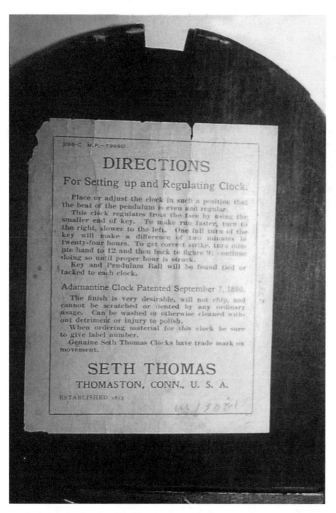

Seth Thomas adamantine (mahogany finish) mantel clock, eight-day, time and strike, 9" wide, 9-1/2" high; $295.

Label on the back of Seth Thomas tambour mantel clock.

Seth Thomas adamantine brown finished mantel clock with four marbleized columns, gilded feet and lion heads, eight-day, time and strike, 19" wide, 11-1/2" high; $250.

Seth Thomas adamantine brown finished mantel clock with four marbleized columns, gilded feet and lion heads, eight-day, time and strike, 16" wide, 12" high; $350.

Seth Thomas adamantine ivory finished mantel clock with six columns, gilded feet and lion heads, eight-day, time and strike, 17-1/2" wide, 11-1/2" high; $300.

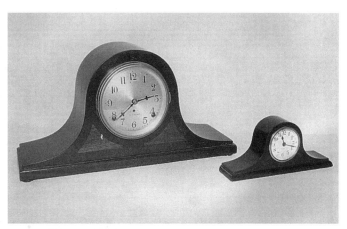

Seth Thomas mahogany tambour shelf clock, eight-day, time only, spring driven, 18" wide, 9-1/2" high; $150. Seth Thomas "Camden" black enameled wooden case tambour shelf clock, eight-day, time only, spring driven, $110.

Seth Thomas adamantine mottled gold finish mantel clock, brass dial, eight hour time and strike, 17" wide, 12" high; $300. A label on back states that this clock was made especially for a company in Rockford, Illinois.

Seth Thomas wooden case mantel clock with celluloid veneer, called adamantine, circa 1902-1917, eight-day, time and strike, spring driven, 9" wide, 10" high; $100. Seth Thomas wooden case mantel clock with celluloid veneer, circa 1902-1917, eight-day, time and strike, spring driven, 8-1/2" wide, 11" high; $100.

Seth Thomas "Sonora" chime, eight bell mahogany shelf clock with inlay, eight-day, time and strike, spring driven, 10" wide, 14" high; $550.

Seth Thomas "Mercury" marbleized wooden mantel clock with gilded decorations, eight-day, time with hour and half-hour chimes, spring driven, 13-1/2" wide, 11" high; $200.

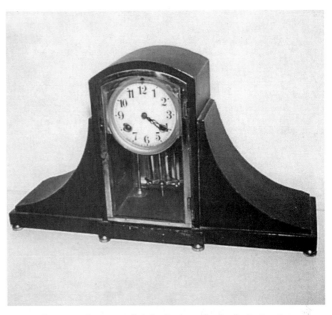

Unknown maker, miniature metal mantel clock, corner columns, time only, 4-1/2" wide, 4" high; $115.

Waterbury mahogany finished mantel clock, imitation mercury pendulum, glass door with brass frame, eight-day, time and strike, 6-1/2" wide, 9-1/2" high; $275.

Waterbury mahogany round top shelf clock, circa 1930, eight-day, time and strike, spring driven, 9" wide, 11-1/2" high; $95.

Ansonia "Minerva" metal mantel clock, circa 1894, with seated lady on top, gilded case, porcelain dial, open escapement, time and strike, 11" wide, 16-1/2" high; $500.

Ansonia "Cygnet" metal mantel clock, circa 1906, with cherub on top holding a wreath, Syrian bronze finish, porcelain dial, eight-day, time and strike, 7-1/2" wide, 12-3/4" high; $450.

Ansonia metal mantel clock with white marbleized case, gilt decorations and copper face, eight-day, time and strike, 11" wide, 18-1/2" high; $500.

Ansonia metal mantel clock with Syrian bronze finish, porcelain dial, open escapement, eight-day, time and strike, 11" wide, 17-1/2" high; $600.

Ansonia iron front shelf clock, circa 1880, eight-day, time only, spring driven, 10-1/2" wide, 12-1/2" high; $300.

Ansonia brass finished metal shelf clock with cherub figure on top, circa 1884, 30-hour time and strike, spring driven, 7-1/2" wide, 13" high; $325.

Jennings Brothers, Bridgeport, Connecticut, gilded metal shelf clock (back left) with cherub decorations on top and porcelain dial, patent 1891, 30-hour, time only, spring driven, 4-1/2" wide, 6-1/2" high; $150. Unknown maker, black metal shelf clock (back right) with porcelain dial, 30-hour, time only, spring driven, 3-1/2" wide, 5" high; $125. Waterbury gilded metal shelf clock (front) with tin can movement, 30-hour, time only, spring driven, 8" wide, 10" high; $150.

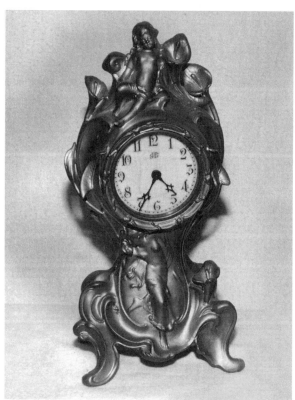

Jennings Brothers metal shelf clock with porcelain dial, 30-hour, time only, spring driven, 6" wide, 13" high; $160.

F. Kroeber brass washed shelf clock, patented May 28, 1878, 30-hour, time and alarm, 5" wide, 7" high; $200.

*Lux metal shelf clock, 30-hour, time only, spring driven, 4-1/2"
wide, 5-1/2" high; $45.*

*New Haven metal front shelf clock with cupid figure,
4-1/2" wide, 7" high; $130.*

*New Haven copper washed metal shelf clock with porcelain dial, eight-day, time only,
spring driven, 5" wide, 8" high; $100.*

Parker iron front shelf clock with visible escapement (on top of clock), 30-hour, time only, 6" high; $1,000. Parker iron front shelf clock with visible escapement (on bottom of clock), 30-hour, time only, 6" high; $1,000.

New Haven iron case shelf clock with brass finish, 30-hour, time only, spring driven, 3" wide, 6" high; $95.

Parker Clock Company metal front mantel clocks, cupids carrying clocks, gilded cast iron cases, 30-hour, time only, Left clock, 6-1/2" high; $450. Right clock, 5-1/2" high; $400.

Regent Manufacturing Company, Chicago, metal shelf clock with tin can movement, 30-hour, time only, spring driven, 11" wide, 12" high; $100.

A.L. Swift, Chicago, metal stove top clock, 30-hour, time only, spring driven, 8" wide 10" high; $125.

E.N. Welch brass washed shelf clock with open escapement, 30-hour, time only, spring driven, 5" wide, 7" high; $200. E.N. Welch brass washed shelf clock with lever movement, 30-hour, time only, 6-1/2" wide, 8" high; $200.

Unknown maker, copper washed metal shelf clock, patented December 15, 1908, 30-hour, time only, spring driven, 6" wide, 9-1/2" high; $100.

Unmarked metal front mantel clock, porcelain and brass dial, gilded case, 30-hour, time only, 3" wide, 4" high; $1325.

Unmarked metal front mantel clock, patented Feb. 6, 1904, brass finish, time only, 7-1/2" wide, 11" high; $135.

Unmarked metal front mantel clock with four frogs, one singing, two playing instruments and one sitting at the base of cast iron case, 30-hour, time only, 9-1/2" wide, 12" high; $250.

Waterbury shelf clock with copper designs on silver-plated case, 30-hour, time only, spring driven, 4" wide, 3" high; $55.

Ansonia oak shelf clock, brass dial, incised and applied decorations, eight-day, time and strike, 12-1/2" wide, 17" high; $300.

Ansonia oak shelf clock, dated 1882, eight-day, time and strike, spring driven, 13-1/2" wide, 14" high; 5" dial; $300.

Ansonia oak shelf clock, circa 1895, eight-day, time and strike, spring driven, 14" wide, 23-1/2" high; $200.

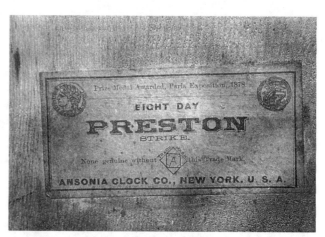

Label from Ansonia "Preston" oak shelf clock.

Ansonia "Preston" oak shelf clock, with label reading, "Prize medal awarded, Paris Exposition, 1878," eight-day, time and strike, spring driven, 13-1/2" wide, 14" high, 5" dial; $300.

Close-up of works from Ansonia "Preston" oak shelf clock showing patent, June 18, 1882.

Ansonia "Trivoli" oak shelf clock, pressed and applied decorations, brass dial, patented June 18, 1882, eight-day, time and strike, 11-1/2" wide, 15" high; $275.

Ansonia "Dalton" oak shelf clock, circa 1885, incised designs, eight-day, time and strike, 12" wide, 23" high; $275.

Ansonia oak shelf clock, circa 1880, pressed designs, eight-day, time and strike, 15" wide, 23" high; $295.

W.L. Gilbert "Egypt" oak shelf clock (part of the Egyptian series), pressed designs, eight-day, time and strike, 17" wide, 25" high; $300

W.L. Gilbert "Mogul" oak shelf clock (part of the Egyptian series), circa 1895, pressed design, eight-day, tie, strike and alarms, 16" wide, 24" high; $300.

W.L. Gilbert "Pasha" oak shelf clock (part of the Egyptian series), circa 1905, pressed designs, eight-day, time, strike and alarm, 15-1/2" wide, 25" high; $300.

W.L. Gilbert "Pyramid" oak shelf clock (part of the Egyptian series), pressed designs, eight-day, time and strike, 15-1/2" wide, 24" high; $300.

Label from W.L. Gilbert "Lion" oak shelf clock.

W.L. Gilbert "Lion" oak shelf clock, circa 1890, eight-day, time and strike, spring driven, 14" wide, 16" high; $165.

W.L. Gilbert "Long Branch" oak shelf clock, eight-day, time and strike, spring driven, 15-1/2" wide, 29" high, 7" dial; $800.

Label from W.L. Gilbert "Long Branch" oak shelf clock.

W.L. Gilbert "Navy Number 27" pressed oak shelf clock, circa 1880, eightday, time and strike, spring driven, 15" wide, 24" high; $225.

W.L. Gilbert "Nebo" oak shelf clock, incised designs, eight-day, time, strike and alarm, 11-1/2" wide, 22" high; $500.

W.L. Gilbert oak shelf clock, circa 1890, incised carving, eight-day, time and strike, 14" wide, 22" high; $275.

W.L. Gilbert oak shelf clock, circa 1901, pressed designs, eight-day, time and strike, 15-1/2" wide, 23" high; $245.

W.L. Gilbert Mission-style oak shelf clock with slag glass flanking dial, dated 1913 on works, eight-day, time and strike, spring driven, 20" wide, 6" deep, 13" high; $275.

E. Ingraham "Post" oak shelf clock, circa 1910, incised designs and applied decorations, eight-day, time and strike, 15" wide, 23" high; $275.

E. Ingraham oak shelf clock, pressed designs, eight-day, time, strike, and alarm, 15" wide, 22" high; $225.

Jerome & Co. mahogany shelf clock, time and strike with alarm. No Price.

E. Ingraham pressed oak shelf clock (left), circa 1880, eight-day, time and strike, spring driven, 14" wide, 19-1/2" high, 5-1/2" dial; $205. Ansonia pressed oak shelf clock, circa 1880, eight-day, time and strike, spring driven, 15" wide, 24" high, 5-1/2" dial; $225.

E. Ingraham miniature oak Mission-style shelf clock, brass hands and numbers on dial, eight-day, time only, spring drive, 6" wide, 14-3/4" high; $295.

Lux oak shelf clock, octagon face, brass dial, 8" wide, 7-1/2" high; $95.

New Haven oak shelf clock with side mirrors, pressed designs, eight-day, time, strike and alarm, 16" wide, 24" high; $450.

George B. Owen oak shelf clock, patented June 17, 1862, time and strike, spring driven, 8" wide, 10-1/2" high; $250.

Sessions oak shelf clock, circa 1880, pressed designs, eight-day time and strike, 15" wide, 23" high; $300.

Sessions oak shelf clock, circa 1910, Mission-style with brass Arabic numerals, eight-day, time only, 8" wide, 14-1/2" high; $175.

Seth Thomas "Number 2" oak kitchen clock, brass decorations, eight-day, time, strike and alarm, 15" wide, 23-1/2" high; $350.

Seth Thomas "Cambridge" oak shelf clock (part of the College series), incised carving and applied decorations, eight-day, time, strike, and alarm 14" wide, 22-1/2" high; $250.

Seth Thomas "New York" oak shelf clock (part of the College series), incised carving and applied decorations, eight-day, time, strike, and alarm, 14" wide, 23" high; $300.

Seth Thomas "Yale" oak shelf clock, (part of the College series), incised carving and applied decorations, eight-day, time, strike, and alarm, 15" wide, 23" high; $250.

Seth Thomas oak shelf clock, eight-day, time, strike and alarm, spring driven; 15" wide, 25-1/2" high; $250.

Seth Thomas oak shelf clock, circa 1880-1890, eight-day, time, strike, and alarm, spring driven, 14" wide, 23-1/2" high; 5" dial; $225. Seth Thomas walnut shelf clock, circa 1880-1890, time, strike and alarm, spring driven, 14" wide, 23-1/2" high, 5" dial; $225. Note that both cases are identical with the exception of the glass tablets.

Seth Thomas oak shelf clock, applied metal decorations, eight-day, time, strike, and alarm, 15" wide, 23" high; $275.

Seth Thomas oak shelf clock, applied metal decorations, eight-day, time, strike, and alarm, 15" wide, 22-1/2" high; $275.

Seth Thomas oak shelf clock, applied metal decorations, eight-day, time, strike, and alarm, 14-1/2" wide, 23" high; $275.

Waterbury "Felix" oak shelf clock, circa 1910, incised carving, eight-day, time, strike, and alarm, 15" wide, 22" high; $300.

Waterbury "Mansfield" oak shelf clock, circa 1890, incised carving and applied decorations, 15" wide, 21-1/2" high; $250.

Waterbury oak shelf clock, circa 1890, eight-day, time and strike, spring driven; 15" wide, 21" high; $225.

Waterbury oak shelf clock, incised carving and applied decorations, simple calendar attachment, eight-day, time and strike, 15" wide, 22" high; $550.

Waterbury oak shelf clock, circa 1899, applied copper decorations, including moose head near top, eight-day, time and strike, 15" wide, 22" high; $265.

American Clock Company "Parlor" walnut shelf clock, eight-day, time and strike, spring driven, 15" wide, 24-1/2" high, 5" dial; $900.

Ansonia "Berkeley" walnut parlor shelf clock, notation on label, "Prize medal awarded at the Paris Exposition, 1878," eight-day, time and strike, spring driven, 15-1/2" wide, 22-1/2" high; $200.

Ansonia "Britannic" walnut shelf clock, patented June 13, 1882, 30-hour, time and strike, 11" wide, 19-1/2" high, 6" dial; $150.

Ansonia "Fifth Avenue" walnut shelf clock, eight-day, time and strike, spring driven, 17" wide, 25" high, 5" dial; $600.

Ansonia "Harwich" cherry shelf clock, circa 1895, open escapement, ceramic dial, time and strike, 12" high; $225.

Ansonia "The Herald" enameled wooden case, time and strike, 9-1/2" wide 16" high; $250.

Ansonia "Mobile" walnut parlor shelf clock, circa 1910, glass sides, circa 1910, incised carving, eight-day, time and strike, 20" high; $525.

Ansonia walnut stained case with hand painted leather panels, open escapement, eight-day, time and strike, 16" wide, 17-1/2" high; $550.

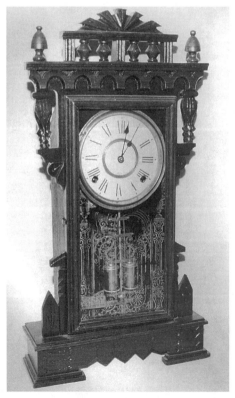

Ansonia walnut shelf clock with imitation mercury pendulum, eight-day, time and strike, spring driven, 12" wide, 22" high; $325.

Ansonia walnut shelf clock, eight-day, time and strike, spring driven, 14" wide, 22" high; $225.

Ansonia walnut shelf clock with side mirrors and metal figures, eight-day, time, strike and alarm, spring driven, 14" wide, 21-1/2" high; 5" dial; $700.

Ansonia oak shelf clock with mirror sides and metal figures, circa 1880, eight-day, time and strike, spring driven, 16-1/2" wide, 24" high, 5" dial; $600. W.L. Gilbert walnut simple calendar shelf clock with mirror sides and metal figures, eight-day, time and strike, spring driven, 16-1/2" wide, 24" high, 5" dial; $600. Note the similarity between these two cases attributed to different clockmakers.

Ansonia black case shelf clock, 30-hour, alarm, 7-1/2" wide, 10-1/2" high; $100. Ansonia white shelf clock, 30-hour, time and alarm, 7-1/2" wide, 10-1/2" high; $110.

Ansonia rosewood Gothic shelf clock, circa 1878, offset pendulum, time only, 10" high; $135.

Benedict Mfg. Co, mahogany shelf clock, medallion below dial, time only, 3-1/2" wide, 4" high; $75.

Congress walnut cottage shelf clock, circa 1880, eight-hour, tie only, 12" high; $150.

W.L, Gilbert "Amphion" walnut parlor shelf clock, etched beveled mirrors, mirror pendulum, applied decorations, Lincoln drape silk screening on door, 16-1/2" wide, 25" high; $2,000.

W.L. Gilbert "Attal" walnut parlor shelf clock, incised carvings, eight-day, time, strike, and alarm, 20-1/2" high; $325.

W.L. Gilbert "Dacca" walnut shelf clock (left), circa 1880, eight-day, time and strike, spring driven, 12" wide, 21-1/2" high, 5" dial; $225. W.L. Gilbert "Nebo" walnut shelf clock, circa 1880, eight-day, time, strike, and alarm, spring driven, 11-1/2" wide, 22" high, 5" dial; $250.

W.L. Gilbert "Forest" walnut shelf clock (left), eight-day, time, strike, and alarm, spring driven, 16" wide, 25" high; $800. Ansonia "Monarch" walnut shelf clock, eight-day, time and strike, spring driven, 15-1/2" wide, 25" high; $800.

W.L. Gilbert "Medea" walnut shelf clock (left), eight-day, time strike, and alarm, spring driven, 13" wide, 20" high, 5" dial; $250. E. Ingraham walnut shelf clock, eight-day, time, strike, and alarm, 16" wide, 24" high; 5" dial; $275

W.L. Gilbert "Occident" oak shelf clock with walnut panels, made for Columbian Exposition of 1893, mirror sides and replaced brass figures, eight-day, time and strike, spring driven, 16" wide, 23-1/2" high; $700.

Close-up of pendulum from W.L. Gilbert "Occident" shelf clock.

W.L. Gilbert "Pandia" walnut shelf clock (left), eight-day, time, strike, and alarm, spring driven, 14" wide, 22" high; 5" dial; $450. W.L. Gilbert "Keystone" rosewood shelf clock, eight-day, time and strike, spring driven, 12-1/2" wide, 18" high; $250.

W.L. Gilbert "Walnut Crown" walnut shelf clock, eight-day, time and strike, spring driven, 14" wide, 20" high; $400.

W.L. Gilbert rosewood shelf clock, circa 1860, spring driven, 13" wide, 19-1/2" high; $250.

W.L. Gilbert walnut-stained shelf clock, eight-day, time, strike, and alarm, spring driven, 13-1/2" wide, 20" high; $225.

W.L. Gilbert mahogany round top shelf clock, circa 1875, eight-day, time and strike, spring driven, 10-1/2" wide, 17-1/2" high; $200.

W.L. Gilbert walnut shelf clock, circa 1870, eight-day, time, strike, and alarm, spring driven, 14" wide, 22" high; $450.

W.L. Gilbert rosewood veneered shelf clock, circa 1870-1880, eight-day, time, bell strike, and alarm; $175.

W.L. Gilbert walnut shelf clock, eight-day, time, strike and alarm, spring drive, 14" wide, 20" high; $400.

E. Ingraham walnut parlor shelf clock, incised carving and applied decorations, sharp Gothic style, eight-day, time, strike, and alarm, 22" high; $265.

E. Ingraham walnut parlor shelf clock, circa 1890, incised carving, eight-day, time, strike, and alarm, 15" wide, 21" high; $225.

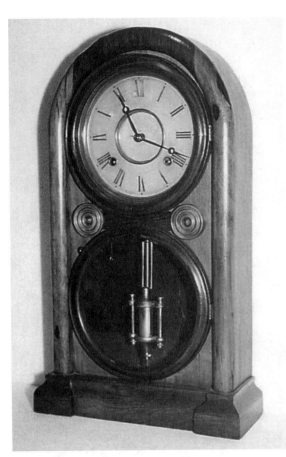

E. Ingraham walnut parlor shelf clock, circa 1895, applied decorations, ionic style, eight-day, time and strike, 22" high; $400.

E. Ingraham rosewood round top shelf clock, eight-day, time and strike, spring driven, 11" wide, 18 " high; $200.

E. Ingraham oak shelf clock, eight-day, time and strike, spring driven, 14-3/4" wide, 22" high; $175. Ansonia "Beaver" walnut shelf clock with notation on label, "Prize medal awarded at Paris Exposition, 1878," eight-day, time and strike, spring driven, 14-1/2" wide, 23-1/2" high; $200.

E. Ingraham, walnut and rosewood shelf clock, patented Sept. 30, 1862, time and strike, 10-1/2" wide, 14-1/2" high; $425.

E. Ingraham walnut shelf clock, circa 1880, eight-day, time and strike, spring driven, 14-1/2" wide, 21" high; $200.

Jerome & Co., New Haven, Connecticut walnut shelf clock, circa 1855, ebony trim, 30-hour, time and strike, 11-1/2" wide, 16-1/2" high; $225.

F. Kroeber "Chalet" walnut parlor shelf clock, circa 1887, pendulum cover removed to expose pendulum, eight-day, time and strike, 17-1/2" high; $265.

F. Kroeber "Dictator" rosewood parlor shelf clock, circa 1882, 30-hour, time and strike, 17" high; $175.

F. Kroeber "Fearless" walnut parlor shelf clock, circa 1887, incised carving, 30-hour, time and strike, 18" high; $250.

F. Kroeber "Galena" walnut parlor shelf clock, circa 1874, incised carving, applied burl decorations, pewter trim, eight-day, time and strike, 23" high; $440.

F. Kroeber "Kansas" walnut parlor shelf clock, circa 1881, carved drop and upright finials, eight-day, time and strike, 20" high; $425.

F. Kroeber "Langtry" walnut parlor shelf clock, incised carving, side pillars and top finials, eight-day, time and strike, 9" wide, 23" high; $21,200.

F. Kroeber, "Library" walnut parlor shelf clock, burled walnut, applied decorations, indicator pendulum, eight-day, time and strike, 18" wide, 24" high; $1,800.

F. Kroeber "Mariposa" walnut parlor shelf clock, crystal pendulum bob, eight-day, time and strike, 16" wide, 22-1/2" high; $750.

F. Kroeber "Occidental" walnut parlor shelf clock, circa 1887, mirror sides with brass statues, applied brass decorations, incised carving, turned side columns, cut glass star bob, eight-day, time and strike, 25" high; $800.

F. Kroeber "Rambler" walnut parlor shelf clock, circa 1890, incised carving, Jacob's patent "Slow and fast" on pendulum, eight-day, time and strike, 11" wide, 20" high; $325.

F. Kroeber walnut parlor shelf clock, circa 1882, incised carving and applied decorations, eight-day, time and strike, 21" high; $225.

New Haven "Corsair" oak shelf clock, eight-day, time, strike, and alarm, spring driven, 17" wide, 23-1/2" high; 5" dial; $900.

New Haven "Tuscan" rosewood shelf clock, eight-day, time and strike, 10-1/2" wide, 17-1/2" high; $475.

New Haven rosewood veneered shelf clock, 30-hour, time, strike, and alarm, spring driven, 9-1/2" wide, 13-1/2" high; $195.

New Haven walnut shelf clock, incised lines and applied decorations, eight-day, time and strike, 14" wide, 21-1/2" high; $225.

New Haven walnut shelf clock, circa 1865-1870, 30-hour, time, strike, and alarm, spring driven, 12-1/2" wide, 22" high; $300.

New Haven walnut shelf clock, eight-day, time and strike, spring driven, 14" wide, 23" high; $300.

Seth Thomas "Albany" walnut parlor shelf clock, applied decorations, eight-day, time, strike, and alarm, 11" wide, 20-1/2" high; $325.

Seth Thomas "Atlanta" parlor shelf clock, side pillars with gilt trim, eight-hour, time and strike, 12-1/2" wide, 20" high; $275.

Seth Thomas "Chicago" walnut and mahogany round top shelf clock, circa 1875, eight-day, time and strike, spring driven, 10-1/2" wide, 17-1/2" high; $335.

Seth Thomas "Garfield" walnut shelf clock, eight-day, time and strike, weight driven, 15-1/2" wide, 30" high, 8" dial, $750.

Seth Thomas "Norfolk" walnut parlor shelf clock, circa 1890, incised carving, eight-hour, time, strike, and alarm, 12" wide, 19-1/2" high; $325.

Seth Thomas "Tacoma" walnut parlor shelf clock, circa 1870, incised carving, winders under dial, eight-day, time and strike, 23" high; $350.

Seth Thomas stained parlor shelf clock, circa 1890, incised carving and railing on top, eight-day, time, strike, and alarm, 13" wide, 21" high; $450.

Seth Thomas walnut shelf clock, 30-hour, time, strike, and alarm, spring driven, 12" wide, 15-1/2" high; $145.

Seth Thomas rosewood shelf (bedroom) clock, circa 1855, 30-hour, time only and alarm, spring driven, 7-1/2" wide, 9-1/2" high; $165.

Seth Thomas rosewood cottage shelf clock, circa 1920, time and strike, 13" high; $150.

Seth Thomas mahogany flat top shelf clock, circa 1866-1870 (Plymouth Hollow label), Geneva stops to prevent over-winding, eight-day, time and strike, 11-1/2" wide, 15-1/2" high; $200.

Waterbury "Cottage No. 1" mahogany shelf clock, 30-hour, time and strike, 8" wide, 11-3/4" high; $225.

Waterbury "Melrose" walnut parlor clock, circa 1881, incised carving, movement is stamped with Waterbury patent, Sept. 22, 1874, eight-day, time and strike, 12-1/2" wide, 21" high; $250.

Waterbury walnut parlor shelf clock, incised carving, sandwich glass pendulum, 30-hour, time and strike, 12" wide, 18-1/2" high; $200.

E.N. Welch, "The Boss" walnut parlor shelf clock, circa 1881, incised carving, 12-1/2" wide, 20" high; $175.

E.N. Welch "Dandelion" walnut parlor shelf clock, incised carving, eight-day, time, strike, and alarm, 10" wide, 17-1/2" high; $200.

E.N. Welch "Dolaro" walnut parlor shelf clock, circa 1885, incised carving, eight-day, time, strike and alarm, 14" wide, 22-1/2" high; $350.

E.N. Welch "Eclipse" walnut parlor shelf clock, incised carving, eight-day, time, strike and alarm, 15-1/2" wide, 24" high. Originally this clock was a wall hanger, but it was so successful it was changed to a shelf clock. For a while it was a premium for the Metropolitan Mfg., New York; $400.

E.N. Welch "Empress" rosewood shelf clock, circa 1875, eight-day, time and strike, 10-1/2" wide, 16" high; $250.

E.N. Welch "Empress VP" mahogany shelf clock, simulated mercury pendulum, eight-day, time and strike, 11-1/2" wide, 17-3/4" high; $275.

E.N. Welch "Gerster VP" (from Patti Series) walnut shelf clock, circa 1890, eight-day, time and strike, spring driven, 12" wide, 20" high, 5" dial; $1,000.

E.N. Welch "Handel" walnut parlor shelf clock, incised carving, applied decorations, "ENW" embossed on pendulum, eight-day, time and strike, 14" wide, 23" high; $300.

E.N. Welch "Judic" (from Patti Series) walnut shelf clock (left), circa 1890, eight-day, time and strike, spring driven, 12" wide, 20" high, 5" dial; $1,000. E.N. Welch "Scachi" (from Patti Series) walnut shelf clock, circa 1875, eight-day, time and strike, spring driven, 12" wide, 20" high, 5" dial; $1,000.

E.N. Welch "Iowa Model" walnut shelf clock with imitation mercury pendulum, eight-day, time and strike, spring driven, 16" wide, 24" high; $900.

E.N. Welch "Litta" walnut parlor shelf clock, incised carving, glass center pendulum, eight-day, time and strike, 16" wide, 23-1/2" high; $350.

E.N. Welch "Lucca" rosewood shelf clock, circa 1870, eight-day, time and strike, spring driven, 14" wide, 23" high; $700.

E.N. Welch "Nanon" walnut parlor shelf clock, circa 1890, incised carving, sandwich glass pendulum, eight-day, time and strike, 15-1/2" wide, 22" high; $400.

E.N. Welch "Pepite" walnut parlor shelf clock, circa 1887, incised carving, sandwich glass pendulum and applied decorations, eight-day, time and strike, 14" wide, 23" high; $350.

E.N. Welch "Roze" walnut parlor shelf clock, incised carving and applied decorations, eight-day, time and strike, 13-1/2" wide, 21" high; $325.

E.N. Welch "Scachi" walnut parlor clock (named after Italian operatic soprano), 1884-1893, incised carving, finials, Patti movement, eight-day, time and strike, 12" wide, 19-3/4" high; $1,100.

E.N. Welch "Titiens" walnut parlor shelf clock (named after German soprano, Theresa Titiens), 1877-1884, finials, decorative turnings on stiles, porcelain dial, B.B. Lewis 30-day movement, time only, 16" wide, 23-1/2" high; $2,00.

E.N. Welch "The Tulip" walnut parlor shelf clock, incised carving, 13" wide, 19-1/2" high; $275.

E.N. Welch "Tycon" walnut parlor shelf clock, incised carving, sandwich glass pendulum, eight-day, time and strike, 14" wide, 23" high; $400.

E.N. Welch walnut parlor shelf clock, incised carving, applied decorations, eight-day, time, strike and alarm, 14" wide, 21" high; $275.

E.N. Welch walnut parlor shelf clock, incised carving, side columns, eight-day, time and strike, 12" wide, 22" high; $350.

E.N. Welch mahogany shelf clock, patented 1868, 30-hour, time and strike, spring driven, 10-1/2" wide, 14" high; $145.

E.N. Welch walnut shelf clock, eight-day, time and strike, spring driven, 15" wide, 23" high; $350.

E.N. Welch walnut shelf clock, circa 1880, eight-day, time and strike, spring driven, 13-1/2" wide, 23" high; 5" dial; $400.

E.N. Welch rosewood shelf clock, circa 1875, applied decorations, time and strike, and alarm, 12" wide, 19" high; $375.

Collection of nine Welch sandwich glass pendulums. These pendulums have been reproduced. Reproductions sell for around $20; original pendulums sell for $80-$120.

Welch, Spring & Co. "Cary" rosewood parlor clock (named after American contralto Annie Louise Cary), four decoratively turned columns, Patti movement, eight-day, time and strike, 12-1/4" wide, 20-1/2" high; $1,400.

Welch, Spring & Co. "Gerster" walnut parlor clock (named after Hungarian soprano Etelka Gerster), four decoratively turned columns, Patti movement, eight-day, time and strike, 12-1/2" wide, 18-1/2" high; $1,400.

Welch, Spring & Co. "Hauck" walnut parlor shelf clock, incised carving, eight-day, time and strike, 14" wide, 22-1/2" high; $350.

Welch, Spring & Co. "The Patti" rosewood parlor shelf clock (named after Spanish operatic prima donna, Adelina Patti), four decoratively turned columns, glass sides, half-hour strike, eight-day time and strike, 12-1/4" wide, 18-3/4" high; $1,400.

Welch, Spring & Co. "Patti N. 2 VP" or "The Baby Patti" rosewood parlor shelf clock, circa 1889, four decoratively turned pillars, eight-day, time only, double spring, 7-1/2" wide, 10-1/2" high; $3,600.

Welch, Spring & Co. stained parlor shelf clock, incised carving, pendulum reads "E.N.W.," eight-day, time and strike, 12-1/2" wide, 21" high; $300.

Chapter 10

Novelty Clocks

To be classified as a novelty a clock should have some unique functions in sounding or telling time, as well as a specialized configuration. When the New Haven Clock Company developed "The Best Show Window Attraction Ever Made," it was called the flying pendulum or the "Ignatz" clock. This one-day, time only clock was patented October 9, 1882. People enjoyed watching it in action as the pendulum, a ball on a string, swung from side to side and wound and unwound to outer posts.

Two-timer is the name given to a clock that has a dual function. One example is the combination of a cigar cutter and clock. An illuminated alarm clock that was lit by a match when the alarm rang was also produced. Examples of these novelties are illustrated in this chapter.

"Sambo," "Topsy," and "Continental" were three novelty clocks, produced in the period between 1874 and 1912, which used eye movements. As the pendulum beat, the eyes moved up and down. Cooperating with their maker, Mueller and Son, Bradley and Hubbard made the iron casting of the bodies to these clocks. Also available with moving eyes were a dog, lion, organ grinder and Santa Claus. Some of these clocks have values in excess of one thousand dollars.

Many of the novelty clocks that use animals in their design, like horses, dogs, birds, squirrels and cats are pictured in this chapter. The bodies or cases of these clocks are predominately metal, but some wooden examples can also be found.

An unusual use of the pendulum was developed by the Ansonia Clock Company. Many unique and expensive novelty clocks with dolls on a swinging pendulum were developed. An 1889 catalog shows a clock by the Ansonia Clock Company, named "Jumper # 3," a thirty-hour, time only clock with a 4-inch dial. It is pictured without a stand and measures 15 inches high. Caution must be observed when purchasing any of these pendulum swingers because they have been widely reproduced.

F. Kroeber used this swinging function in two clocks that he developed. A child swinging to and from on the pendulum rod is shown on both clocks. One of the clocks is bronzed while the other is a combination of pot metal and walnut. Both were manufactured in the late 1870s. Mastercrafters produced electric novelty clocks, often depicting children swinging on the pendulums, during the 20th century.

It is fascinating to read about the unusual novelty clocks that were marketed in the late 1800s and early 1900s. A burglar and fire-detective alarm clock was produced through the combined efforts of Seth Thomas, Plymouth Hollow and G. K. Proctor & Co. It was patented August 7, 1860. A lamp lit up when the alarm sounded. The clock's rosewood case measured 11 1/4 inches high.

An unusual clock brought out by Seth Thomas was a 30-hour ship's bell clock. It had a metal case with a bell beneath and struck ship's bells rather than the hours. Other clock manufacturers who made ship's bell clocks were Waterbury and Chelsea Clock Companies. The latter was probably the largest producer of this type of clock with the widest variety of styles.

Chess is a highly competitive game where two players vie against each other as they seek to win. How long is the thinking interval between moves? Yale Clock Company produced two rectangular tilted clocks on a mutual base to help serious chess players time their moves.

In the early 1900s a slot machine clock with an attractive decorated black wooden case served those who liked to put money in the slot machine. The players who won were few and far between.

Another unusual clock had a translucent milk glass dial. The clock could be hooked on a wall gas cock (the faucet used to turn the gas on and off), which made it possible to read the time at night.

A novelty Hickory-Dickory-Dock clock shows a white mouse running up the clock. The New Haven Clock Company developed five models of this nursery rhyme inspired mouse clock. A Sessions brand clock depicting this same nursery rhyme is illustrated in this chapter.

Two examples of Ferris Wheel clocks that were souvenirs of the Paris 1900 Exposition are pictured in this chapter. These are time only clocks that are nearly 12 inches high. As the clock runs the Ferris Wheel turns.

The Plato clock by Ansonia is an early version of a digital clock according to the collector who owns it. Its inventor, Eugene L. Fitch, patented it in 1902. He called it a time indicator. Time was indicated on this clock by the turning of the numbered leaves. Replicas of this timepiece have been made in Germany.

The Lux Manufacturing Company of Waterbury, Connecticut, began making novelty clocks as a family project prior to World War I. Current events and comic characters often provided the inspiration for their amusing clocks. DeLux and Keebler are two names often found on these clocks.

Some Lux clock examples include the following creations: an animated butcher showing a butcher who chops meat while a cat watches; an organ grinder and monkey, showing the monkey climbing a fence while the man turns the organ crank; and "Happy Days" where two drinkers are seen over a beer barrel.

Manufacturing costs for these novelty clocks were kept to a minimum by the use of synthetic materials. Compressed molded wood and a synthetic marble named "Marblesque" were used in the making of these animated clocks. Lux's pendulettes have been produced in large numbers and show unusual objects being substituted for the pendulums. For example, on the Dixie Boy Pendulette, the boy's necktie swings back and forth and his eyes roll from side to side.

H. J. Davies milk glass wall clocks, circa 1871-74, 30-hour, time only, spring driven, left clock 4" diameter, right clock 5" wide, 7" high; $250 each.

Ansonia plush velvet wall clock with brass decorations and porcelain shield numbers on brass dial, eight-day, time only, two spring driven, 16" diameter; $450.

F. Kroeber "Picture Frame" walnut wall clock with velvet backing and key winds hidden under bezel, eight-day, time and strike, spring driven, 11" wide, 13" high; $500.

Keebler cuckoo pendulette, molded wood, green colored leaves, 30-hour, time only, spring driven, 3-1/2" wide, 6" high; $55.

Keebler pendulette, molded wood, spread winged eagle at the top, green leaves, 30-hour, time only, spring driven, 4" wide, 5" high; $45.

Keebler cuckoo pendulette, molded wood, 30-hour, time only, spring driven, 4" wide, 5" high; $45.

Keebler "Coo-Coo" clock in original box, never used, molded wood, 30-hour, time only, 4-1/2" wide, 7" high; $150.

Keebler cuckoo pendulette, molded wood, green leaves and red flowers, bluebird feeds its babies, 30-hour, time only, spring driven, 4" wide, 5" high; $45.

Lux cuckoo pendulette, molded wood, bird sitting on top, 30-hour, time only, spring driven, 4" wide, 6" high; $45.

Lux cuckoo pendulette, molded wood, bird sitting at the top, 30-hour, time only, spring driven, 8-1/2" wide, 11-1/2" high; $200.

Lux cuckoo pendulette, molded wood, bird sitting at the top, 30-hour, time only, spring driven, 4-1/2" wide, 7" high; $55.

Lux cuckoo pendulette, molded wood, green leaves and bluebird, time only, spring drive, 4" wide, 5" high; $45.

Lux cuckoo pendulette with original box marked, "Lux Pendulette Clock—a Novelty Clock by Lux," 30-hour, time only, spring driven, 4" wide, 7" high; $150.

Lux Bird Design10" wide, 19" high; $300. Lux deer head, 10" wide, 19" high; $300. Lux single bird facing left 9" wide, 17" high; $85. Lux single bird facing right, 7" wide, 15" high; $85. All are molded wood cuckoo pendulette wall clocks, 30-hour, time only and spring driven.

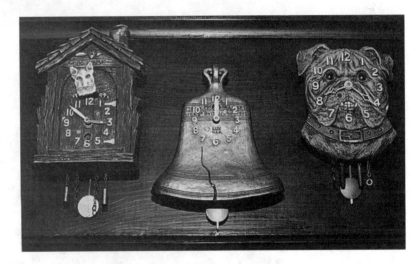

Lux "Dog House," $350. Lux "Liberty Bell," $400. Lux "Bull Dog," $1,800. All are pendulette wall clocks, 30-hour, time only and spring driven.

Lux "Picaninny" wall clock, $800. "Three Scotties" wall clock, $300. "Hungry Dog" wall clock, $400. All are 30-hour, time only, spring driven pendulettes.

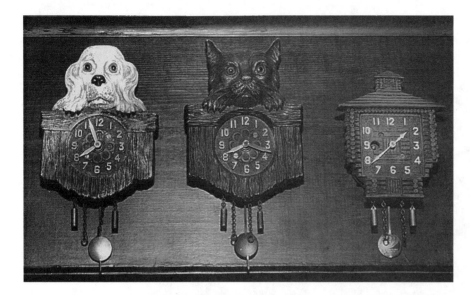

Lux "Dog on a Fence" and "Cat on a Fence" pendulette wall clocks, 30-hour, time only, spring driven; $600 each. Lux "Fort Dearborn" wall clock with "1933 Century of Progress" on pendulum, 30-hour, time only, spring driven; $600.

Lux "Sally Rand" wall clock with "Century of Progress 1933" on pendulum, 30-hour, time only, spring driven; $800. Lux "Christmas Wreath" wall clock, 30-hour, time only, spring driven; $3,500.

Lux "Potted Petunia," $575. Lux "Sunflower," $400. Lux "Clown with Tie," $800. All are pendulette wall clocks, 30-hour, time only and spring driven.

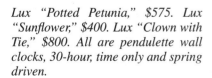

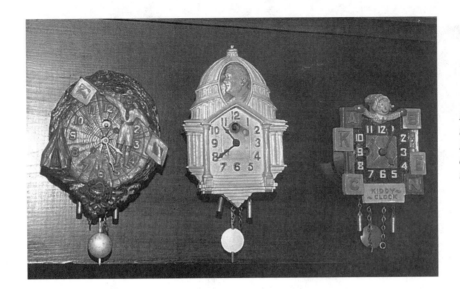

Lux "Boy Scout," $650. Lux "Capitol" clock with FDR on top; $600. Lux "ABC Kiddy Clock," $400. All are pendulette wall clocks, 30-hour, time only and spring driven.

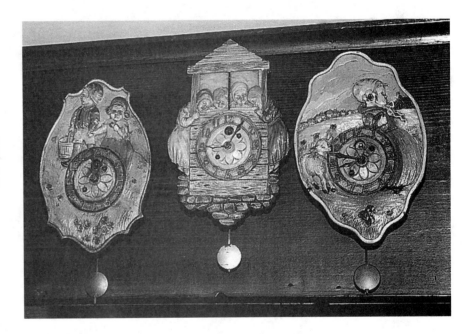

Lux composition wall clocks, Jack and Jill, Pussy in the Well and Mary Had a Little Lamb, 30-hour, time only, spring driven; $1,200 each.

Lux "Shmoo," $200. Lux "Honey Bunny," $350. Lux "Woody Woodpecker," $300. All are pendulette wall clocks, 30-hour, time only and spring driven.

Lux "Golfer," Lux "Country Scene," and Lux "Niagara." All are metal pendulette wall clocks, 30-hour, time only and spring driven; $700 each.

New Haven brass hanging clock with porcelain shield numbers on brass dial, circa 1885, 30-hour, time only, double spring driven, 15" diameter; $650.

New Haven brass wall clock, circa 1875, 30-day, time only, marine movement with two main spring drive and balance wheel control; 8" diameter; $425.

New Haven cannery process clock with "Ayars Machine Company, New Salem, New Jersey" on dial, 15-day, two spring movement, 18" wide, 39" high; $800.

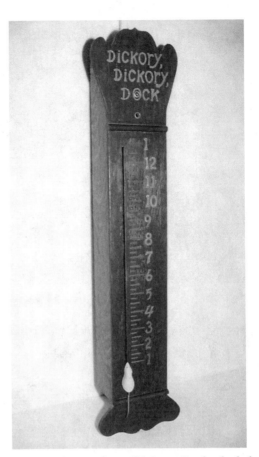

Sessions wooden Dickory, Dickory Dock clock has a white mouse running up and down the time line, eight-day, time only, 35" high; $1,000.

Gain's Reminder clock made by Valley Mfg. Co., Muscatine, Iowa, patented March 15, 1921, 4-1/2" wide, 20" high; $500.

Westclox plastic calico horse wall clock, 30-hour, time only, spring driven; $250.

Ansonia brass novelty clocks, left: "Swing #1" doll, 30-hour, time only, 4" dial, 11-1/2" high; $2,400. Right: "Swing #2" doll, 30-hour, time only, 4" dial, 8" high; $1,500.

Ansonia "Swinging Doll" (moves back and forth as pendulum) shelf clock, 30-hour, time only, spring driven, 7" wide, 8" high; $550.

Ansonia "Jumper #1" 30-hour, time only, 4" dial, 15-1/2" high; $1,800. Right: "Jumper #2" 30-hour, time only, 4" dial, 14-1/2" high; $1,750.

Ansonia metal shelf clock with female figures at each corner, 30-hour, time only, spring driven, 5-1/2" wide, 6" high; $225.

Ansonia Brass & Copper Company illuminated alarm clock operates so that match lights lamp when the alarm, patented by H.J Davis, is tripped, 7-1/2" wide, 17" high; $2,500. Waterbury movement black enameled slot-machine mantel clock, early 1900s, the slot machine was patented in 1908 by Loheide Manufacturing Company and was intended to take $2.50 gold pieces, 14" wide, 10-1/2" high; $1,500.

Ansonia squirrel in a tree, enameled pot metal, 30-hour, time only, 7" wide, 6" high; $700. Right: Ansonia clock in a brass frame featuring two robins, one of which is feeding the babies in a nest, 30-hour, time only, 5-1/2" wide, 7" high; $350.

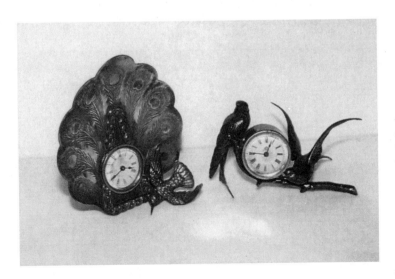

Ansonia "Novelty #23 Peacock" with embossed metal surround and appendages, 30-hour, time only, 2" dial, 7-1/2" high; $700. Right "Novelty #20 Birds" metal, 30-hour, time only, 2" dial, 4-1/2" high; $600.

Ansonia "Train Novelty #44" patented April 23, 1878, 30-hour, time only, 2" dial, 7-3/4" high; $750. Right: Ansonia "Cat Novelty #52" 30-hour, time only, 2" dial, 9" high; $1,100.

Ansonia "Novelty #34" also called "The Advertiser" because there is space for ads above and below the dial, 30-hour, time only, 7" high; $650. Right: Ansonia "Novelty #15" with owl supporting clock, 30-hour, time only, 2" dial, 6" high; $650.

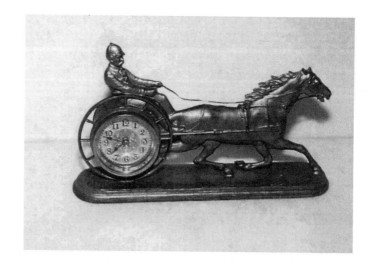

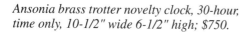

Ansonia brass trotter novelty clock, 30-hour, time only, 10-1/2" wide 6-1/2" high; $750.

Ansonia metal man beating time, 30-hour, time only, 2" dial, 5" high; $1,250. Right: Ansonia "Novelty #48" of children sledding, 30-hour, time only, 6" wide, 6-3/4" high; $1,000.

Ansonia metal novelty clocks with porcelain dials, eight-day, time only. Small figure, $800; large figure; $750.

Ansonia brass Cupid riding a snail, 30-hour, time only, 5" high; $300. Right: Ansonia brass baby holding a fan, 30-hour, time only, 5" high; $475.

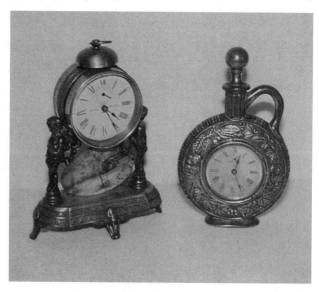

Ansonia "Twins" 30-hour, time only, movement patented March 27, 1877, 3" dial, 10-1/2" high; $600. Right: Ansonia "The Jug" 30-hour, time only, 3" dial, 10" high; $225.

Ansonia cast-iron black enamel novelty mantel clock, with a ship's brass wheel rotating as the escapement moves, seen in 1894 catalog, 15" wide, 18-3/4" high; $2,200.

Ansonia "Eva" novelty shelf clock with brass surround, patented 1892, porcelain dial, beveled mirror, eight-day, time only, 8" wide, 9-1/2" high; $800.

Ansonia "The Sonnet" brass framed novelty shelf clock, with knight's head on velvet background, eight-day, time only, tandem spring drive, 20-1/2" high; $2,000.

Ansonia metal "castle" novelty clock, time only, 14" high; $475.

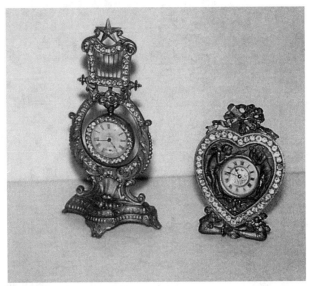

Ansonia brass jeweled novelty clocks. Left: "The Harp" 30-hour, time only, 1-1/2" dial, 9" high; $800. Right: "The Token" porcelain dial, gilt center, two cupids within heart design, 30-hour, time only, 1-1/2" dial, 5-1/2" high; $600.

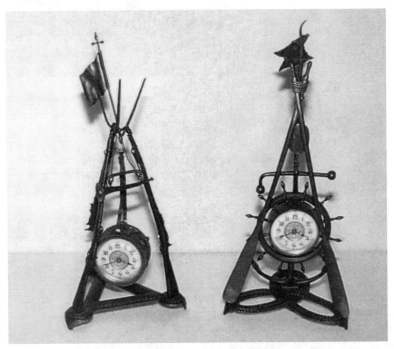

Ansonia metal novelty clocks with jeweled settings. Left: "Army" with rifle supports, antique brass, gilt center, porcelain dial, one-day, time only, 2" dial, 12" high; $900. Right: "Navy" with oar supports, antique brass, gilt center, porcelain dial, one-day, time only, 2" dial, 12" high; $850.

Ansonia metal anchor and ship's wheel novelty clock, time only, 9" high; $700. Right: Ansonia metal novelty clock with a sailor sitting on a rope under the clock which is supported by a pair of oars, time and alarm, 8" high; $600.

Ansonia metal "ship" novelty clocks with cupid figure on each, 30-hour, time only. The middle ship is 13" high and other two are 9" high; $375.

Ansonia metal novelty clocks. Left: "Simmons Liver Regulator" on horseshoe surround, 30-hour, time only, 6" high; $500. Right: "Pearl" 30-hour, time only, 4" diameter dial, 6-1/2" high; $250.

Left: Ansonia Plato Design #2 early digital novelty clock, patented 1903, time only, 6-1/2" high; $650. Right: "Design #4" early digital novelty clock, patented 1903, time only, 6-1/2" high; $650.

Ansonia "Bee" clock shown with its original shipping tin, circa 1890, time only, 2" dial; $150.

Ansonia "Square Pirate" clock with original cardboard box, 4" wide, 4" high; $60.

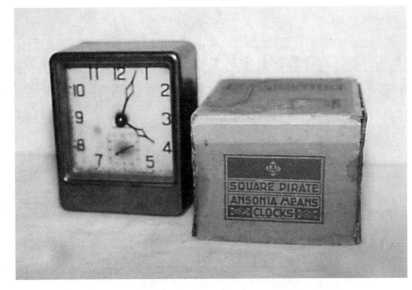

Brewster & Ingraham walnut open case showing its brass east-west movement, 15" diameter; $500.

J.E. Buerk, Boston, made the first time clock, patented 1861, brass with leather case, 3-1/2" diameter; $700.

Darche Manufacturing Company, Chicago, wooden case pool-room timer, circa 1920-30, eight-day, time only, spring driven, 13-1/2" wide, 12" high; $200

W. L. Gilbert wooden religious mass clock, 5" wide, 6" high; $150.

W. L. Gilbert miniature wooden round top shelf clock, patented February 10, 1904, 30-hour, time only, spring driven, 3" wide, 5-1/2" high; $35.

Golden Manufacturing Company, Chicago, copper washed metal case with works by Waterbury, patented 1891, 30-hour, time only, spring driven, 7" high; $250.

Howard Clock Corporation electric "God Bless America" wooden shelf clock, patented 1940, 8-1/2" wide, 8" high; $225.

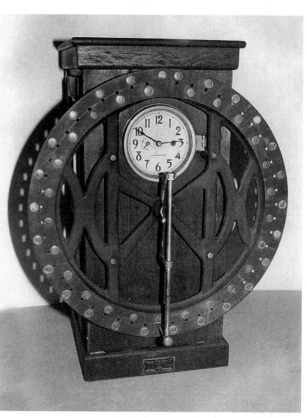

International Business Machine Corporation time clock, patented March 7, 1916, 22" deep, 35" high; $700.

E. Ingraham miniature wooden grandfather shelf clock, 30-hour, time only. spring driven, 11" high; $100.

Kline & Company, New York, "#602" chronometer in a wooden case, circa 1830, fusee operated, 7-1/4" wide, 7-1/2" high; $2,200.

F. Kroeber bronzed novelty clock with Kroeber movement, girl swings to and fro by using Kroeber's double escapement wheel on the pendulum rod, Egyptian lady's head above dial, eight-day, time only, 5" wide, 19" high; $2,000.

F. Kroeber owl novelty clock, glass eyes, 30-hour, time and alarm, 6" wide, 10" high; $475.

F. Kroeber pot metal and walnut "Angel Swing" novelty parlor clock, circa 1876, reconditioned case, eight-day, time only, 19-1/2" high; $2,600.

F. Kroeber "Sheffield" walnut miniature novelty shelf clock, circa 1890, time only, 20" high; $150.

Lux "Happy Days" clock, showing two drinkers standing next to a "3 Point 2" beer barrel, 30-hour, time only, 4" wide, 4" high; $250.

Lux novelty shelf clock, showing fireplace scene with turning spinning wheel, 30-hour, time and alarm, 4-1/2" wide, 5" high; $125.

Lux "Show Boat" clock with paddle wheel that turns, 30-hour, time only, 5" wide, 4-1/2" high; $175.

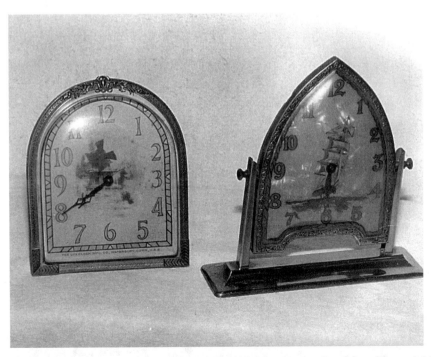

Lux shelf clock with windmill on celluloid dial, 30-hour, time only, spring driven, 4-1/2" wide, 5-1/2" high; $125. Lux shelf clock with Capitol clipper ship on celluloid dial; 30-hour, time only, spring driven-, $125.

Lux Good Luck metal clock featuring a Horse Shoe surrounding the clock, 30-hour, time only, 9" wide, 7-1/2" high; $50.

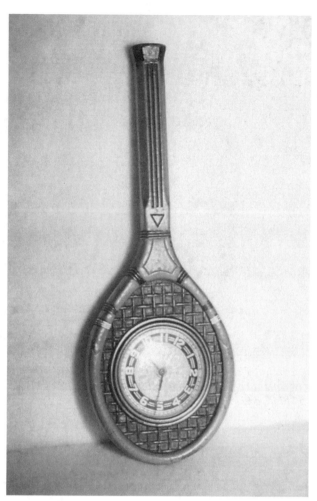

Lux "Tennis Racket" clock, 30-hour, time only, 3" wide, 7-1/2" high; $100.

Lux wooden clock featuring aviator and soldier on blue base, 30-hour, time only, spring drive, 9" wide, 7" high; $800.

Lux composition cat and owl shelf clocks, 30-hour, time only, spring driven, 5-1/2" high; $175 each. Lux composition thermometer, 6" high, (not a clock); $50.

Lux "The Village Mill" composition shelf clock, 30-hour, time only, spring driven, 8" wide, 10-1/2" high; $35.

Lux "The Waiter," "The Drunk," and "The Clown" composition shelf clocks, 30-hour, time only, spring driven, 6-1/2" high; $150 each.

DeLux "Bungalow" composition shelf clock, pictured in 1927 Sears catalog, 30-hour, time only, spring driven, 10-1/2" wide, 6" high; $35. "DeLux" was another name used by Lux on its clocks.

Lux "The Homestead" composition shelf clock, pictured in 1927 Sears catalog, 30-hour, time only, spring driven, 10" wide, 6" high; $35.

Lux metal shelf clock, 30-hour, time only, spring driven, 1 "dial; $35. Lux sailboat shelf clock, 30-hour, time only, spring driven, 8" wide, 10" high; $35. Lux "Louis XVI Art clock," 30-hour, time only, spring driven, 1-3/4" dial, $35.

Lux miniature wooden grandfather shelf clock, 30-hour, time only, spring driven, 10-1/2" high; $125. Lux mirror shelf clock, 30-hour, time only, spring driven, 8" square frame; $40.

Lux cast-iron inkwell shelf clock, 30-hour, time only, spring driven, 8" high; $200.

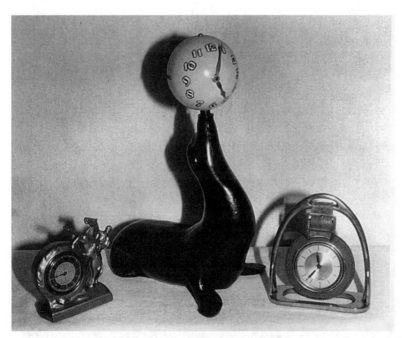

Lux gilded metal shelf clock with man riding horse, 30-hour, time only, spring driven, 4" high; $150. Lux seal and ball metal shelf clock, 30-hour, time only, spring driven, 8" wide, 12" high; $200. English stirrup shelf clock, 30-hour, time only, spring driven, 5" wide, 5" high; $125.

Lux bird in cage metal shelf clock, 30-hour, time only, spring driven, 5" diameter, 7" high; $175.

Lux synthetic marble red elephant shelf clock, 30-hour, time only, spring driven, 7" wide, 6-1/2" high, $125. Lux synthetic marble white elephant shelf clock, 30-hour, time only, spring driven, 7" wide, 6-1/2" high; $125. Ansonia metal elephant shelf clock, 30-hour, time only, spring driven, 9" wide, 9" high; $125. Waterbury metal elephant shelf clock, 30-hour, time only, spring driven, 6-1/2" wide, 5-1/2" high; $125.

Lux Pendulum Stand shelf clock, 30-hour, time only, spring driven, 5-1/2" to 6-1/2" high; $125 each.

Lux "Rotary Calendar Clock" patented 1932, 5" diameter, 5" high, $100.

Lux mystery rotary metal shelf clock in Art Moderne black, 5" diameter, 3" high; $60.

Lux rotary metal tape measure novelty clock, circa 1910, copper finish, time only, 5" diameter; $45.

The top of a shipping crate used for shipping Lux clocks, 26" wide, 15-1/2" high; $100.

Mastercrafters plastic case novelty clock with boy and girl swinging as time ticks, time only; $175.

Mastercrafters electric novelty clocks. Left: animated blacksmith; $85. Right: girl swinging; $165.

Mastercrafters collection of electric novelty clocks, popular in the 1940s. Top row: $125 (girl), $175 (boy and girl); $125 (girl); $100 (bird). Bottom row: $90 (church); $55 (waterfalls); $90 (church chimes) $75 (fireplace).

Minneapolis-Honeywell Regulator Co. combination metal clock and thermometer, eight-day, time only, seven jewel model, 2-1/2" dial, 10" high; $65.

N. Muller's Sons "A Narrow Escape" shelf clock with a cat and mouse on slate, circa 1887, 30-hour, time only, spring driven, 6-3/4" wide, 8-1/2" high; $500.

"Muscatine Timer" by the Hawkeye Clock Company, 30-hour, time only, 4" wide, 6" high; $75.

The Nasco lighter 18-karat, gold-plated pocket clock, 1-1/2" wide, 2" high, $75.

New Haven manufactured (using the Jerome & Company name) "Ignatz" or flying pendulum shelf clock, with A. C. Clausen October 9, 1883, patent movement, 30-hour, time only, hair spring driven, 7" wide, 10-1/2" high; $550.

New Haven "Tip Top Traveler" metal shelf clock, 30-hour, time only, spring driven, 1-3/4" high; $75. New Haven photo easel shelf clock, 30-hour, time only, spring driven, 5-3/4" wide, 8" high; $100.

New Haven ball watch hanging on eagle stand with onyx base, 30-hour, time only, 9" high; $1,100.

New Haven brass dresser clock, porcelain dial, 3" diameter, time only; $100.

Pallwebber's digital pendulum patent used in this walnut novelty shelf clock. There is a second hand and two windows that display the hours and minutes, beveled glass, eight-day, time only, 12" wide, 13" high; $1,000.

Parker & Whipple Company metal shelf clock with porcelain dial (left to right), 30-hour, time only, spring driven, 4-1/2" wide, 6-1/2" high; $150. Parker & Whipple Company metal shelf clock, 30-hour, time only, spring driven, 2" wide, 3" high, $175. Parker & Whipple Company metal shelf clock, patented January 20, 1880, 30-hour, time only, spring driven, 2-1/2" wide, 3" high; $175.

Two animal clocks: Russell & Jones "jockey" silver-plated (left), 30-hour, time only, 7-3/4" wide, 7" high; $600. Jennings Brothers Mfg. Co. bull dog, gilt finish, patented Jan. 13, 1891, Bridgeport, Connecticut, 30-hour, time only, 8" wide, 6" high; $450.

Sentinola kitchen call clock tells when something is done, like a timer, 7-1/2" wide, 7" high; $50.

Sessions "Ballerina" electric clock with walnut stained case and gold-plated figure, patented 1937, 9" wide, 11-1/4" high; $95.

Sessions walnut veneered electric shelf clock, patented 1936, 20" wide, 19" high; $45.

Seth Thomas "Shakespeare Bust" gilded metal shelf clock with porcelain dial, 30-hour, time only, spring driven, 4" wide, 8" high; $175.

Timby Solar walnut novelty shelf clock with a world globe that rotates to indicate the hours, base dial rotates to register the minutes, time only, only 600 of these clocks were made, 14" wide, 27" high: $5,000-$6,000.

United Metal Goods Mfg. Co. Inc. electric carriage novelty clock, patent 1938, 13" wide, 9" high; $95.

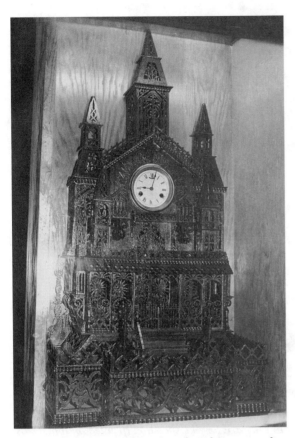

Barnes Smith & Company cigar cutter with attached unknown maker clock that is marked "Yale & Co. Jewelers" on dial, 30-hour, time only, spring driven, 14" high; $1,500. J. Becker & Son "Bonny Jean" cigar cutter with clock movement; $500. King Alfred Cigar cutter with attached Waterbury clock, 30-hour, time only, spring driven, 13" high; $1,500.

Unknown maker, triple towered mahogany cathedral clock, not signed but similar to the handcrafted work of Frank L. & Joseph C. Bily, Spillville, Iowa, eight-day, time only, Lieben marine movement, 19" wide, 11" deep, 36" high; $1,000

Unknown maker, metal Art Deco shelf clock, 7" high, 8-1/2" high; $75.

Unknown maker with Herschede movement American shelf clock, seven jewels, circa 1900, eight-day, time only, 7" diameter; $250.

Unknown maker, metal Ferris Wheel novelty clock, souvenir of the Paris 1900 Exposition (printed on tablet), as the clock runs, the Ferris Wheel turns, time only, 5" wide, 11-1/2" high; $1,000.

Another example of a Ferris Wheel clock – this one with a plain tablet; $1,000.

Maker unknown, three piece set of horses with the center one holding the clock, circa 1890, gold finish, porcelain dial, beveled glass, eight-day, time only, 12" wide, 15-1/2" high; $650.

Unknown maker, electrically operated plastic wind-mill shelf clock with moving blades, circa 1940, time only, 8-1/2" high; $100.

Unknown maker, reproduction of Flying Pendulum novelty clock, original patent date was 1883, 7" wide, 10" high; $100.

Unknown maker, mahogany finished four column novelty shelf clock, porcelain dial, time only, 6-1/2" diameter dial, 13" high; $250.

Unknown maker, brass Masonic emblem novelty desk clock, circa 1910, time only, 6-1/2" high; $190.

Waterbury wooden and metal novelty clock showing boy with saw, patented Jan. 13, 1891, 30-hour, time only, 8-1/2" wide, 10-1/2" high; $650.

Waterbury walnut stained shelf clock with a hand that goes up and down and rotates at the top and bottom to show time on this elongated dial, eight-day, time only, 13" wide, 15" high; $500-$600.

Left E.N. Welch metal suitcase novelty clock, copper washed, 30-hour, time only, 3" wide, 2" high; $450. Waterbury brass finished novelty clock on stand with two black figures, standing by bale of cotton which serves as a match holder, 30-hour, time only, 6" wide, 5" high; $650.

Waterbury miniature brass carriage clock, marked "W.A. Fraser Co., Grain, Chicago," 30-hour, time only, spring driven, 2" wide, 2-1/2" high; $250.

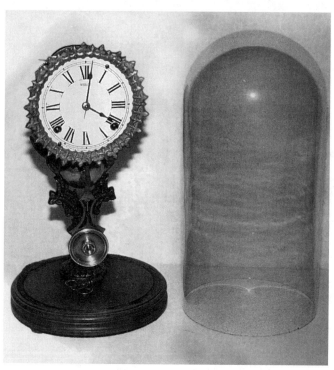

E. N. Welch skeleton shelf clock, with glass dome, late 1800, eight-day, time and strike, spring driven, 9-1/2" diameter, 16" high, no price available.

E.N. Welch "Brigg's Rotary" shelf clock with glass dome, patented by John C. Briggs in 1855, 30-hour, time only, spring driven, 7-1/2" high; $750.

E. N. Welch brass shelf clock with open escapement, patented October 1, 1878, 30-hour, time only, spring driven, 7" wide, 8" high; $150.

E. N. Welch metal suitcase novelty clock, copper finished, 30-hour, time only, 3" wide, 3" high; $300.

E. N. Welch "Rosebud" clock with an angel and flowers inscribed on the brass clock surround, 30-hour, time only, 6" wide, 7" high; $400.

E.N. Welch nickel-plated novelty shelf clock, time only, 3" wide, 2" high; $225. Right: E.N. Welch novelty clock shaped like a watch, souvenir from 1893 Chicago World's Fair, 30-hour, time only, 3" diameter. Inscription on back reads: "Landing of Columbus in America October 12th 1492"; $350.

E. N. Welch jewel novelty clocks. Left: amber, patented 1881, 30-hour, time only, 4" wide, 4" high; $275. Right: crystal, 30-hour, time only, 4" wide, 4" high; $225.

Westclox Big Ben alarm clock, patented 1914; $65.

Western Clock Company, La Salle, Illinois "volunteers" metal shelf clock, showing two men by a thirteen-star flag, 30-hour, time only, spring driven, 10" high; $100. Western Clock Company gilded metal shelf clock with cherub and grotesque figures, patented October 22, 1902, 30-hour, time only, spring driven, 11" high, $50. Ansonia "Croquet players" metal shelf clock, patented April 23, 1878; 30-hour, time only, spring driven; 8" wide, 7-1/2" high; $200. Hawkeye Clock Company, Muscatine, Iowa brass clock and timer combination; 4-1/2" wide, 6" high; $75.

Western Clock Company, La Salle, Illinois, metal horse-shoe on wooden base shelf clock, 30-hour, time only, spring driven, 7-1/2" high; $200.

Yale Clock Company metal shelf clock, patented 1881, 30-hour, time only, spring driven, 2" wide, 3" high; $200.

Year Clock Company, New York, mahogany case novelty clock that runs a year, patented 1903, 4" dial; $650.

Chapter 11

Useful Clock Information

Inventors of Calendar Clocks

Patent Date	Inventor	Residence
May 17, 1853	John H. H. Hawes	Ithaca, N.Y.
Sept. 19, 1854	William H. Atkins and Joseph C. Burritt	Ithaca, N.Y.
Nov. 17, 1857	William H. Atkins and Joseph C. Burritt	Ithaca, N.Y.
Jan 31, 1860	James E. and Eugene M. Mix	Bristol, Conn.
Mar. 5, 1861	Galusha Maranville	Winston, Conn.
Feb. 4, 1862	Benjamin B. Lewis	Bristol, Conn.
April 4, 1862	James E. and Eugene M. Mix	Bristol, Conn.
Jan. 5, 1864	Don J. Mozart, Levi Beach and La Porte Hubbel	New York, N.Y.
June 21, 1864	Benjamin B. Lewis	Bristol, Conn.
April 18, 1865	Henry B. Horton	Ithaca, N.Y.
April 24, 1866	George B. Owen	New York, N.Y.
Aug. 28, 1866	Henry B. Horton	Ithaca, N.Y.
June 25, 1867	Charles M. Clinton and Lynfred Mood	Ithaca, N.Y.
July 2, 1867	Alfonzo Boardman	Forestville, Conn.
Nov. 11, 1867	Charles M. Clinton and Lynfred Mood	Ithaca, N.Y.
Jan. 7, 1868	Josiah K. Seem	Canton, Pa.
June 16, 1868	William A. Terry	Bristol, Conn.
Dec. 29, 1868	Benjamin B. Lewis	Bristol, Conn.
Jan. 25, 1870	William A. Terry	Bristol, Conn.
Dec. 24, 1872	Josiah K. Seem	Macomb, Ill.
July 13, 1875	Alfred A. Cowles	New York, N.Y.
July 13, 1875	William A. Terry	Bristol, Conn.
Feb. 15, 1876	Randal T. Andrews	Thomaston, Conn.
Dec. 5, 1876	Albert Phelps	Ansonia, Conn.
June 19, 1877	Daniel J. Gale	Sheboygan, Wis.
July 31, 1877	Florence Kroeber	Hoboken, N.J.
Nov, 15, 1881	Benjamin B. Lewis	Bristol, Conn.
Dec. 13, 1881	Josiah K. Seem	Macomb, Ill.
June 12, 1883	Benjamin Franklin	Chicago, Ill.
June 19, 1883	James E. Young	Genoa, N.Y.
April 21, 1885	Daniel J. Gale	Sheboygan, Wis.
July 30, 1889	A. F. Wells	Friendship, N.Y.
April 14, 1891	Henry S. Prentiss	New York, N.Y.
Oct. 9, 1894	Charles W. Feishtingfer	Fritztown, Pa.
Nov. 10, 1896	T. W. R. McCabe	Winston, Conn.
July 15, 1902	John I. Peatfield	Arlington, Mass.

Patent Serial Numbers Grouped in 10 Year Periods

Patent Numbers	Years Included	Patent Numbers	Years Included
1-1,464	1836-1839	640,167-945,009	1900-1909
1,465-6,980	1840-1849	945,010-1,326,898	1910-1919
6,981-26,641	1850-1859	1,326,899-1,742,180	1920-1929
26,642-98,459	1860-1869	1,742,181-2,185,169	1930-1939
98,460-223,210	1870-1879	2,185,170-2,492,943	1940-1949
223,211-418,664	1880-1889	2,492,944-2,919,442	1950-1959
418,665-640,166	1890-1899		

Clock Museums

The following listing of clocks can be found at the American Clock and Watch Museum, Bristol, Connecticut. They are listed in chronological order. Other clock museums follow these entries.

1710   English lantern clock made by Henry Webster, London, England.

1711   English clock with inlaid marquetry case by William Troutbeck, Leeds, England.

1750   Cheney-style wood tall clock with movement and dial made in Eastern Connecticut.

1780   A one-day wood movement tall clock in pine case made by Alexander T. Willard, at Ashby, Massachusetts.

1790   Connecticut tall clock in cherry case by Thomas Harland, Norwich, Connecticut.

1790   A tall clock by Benjamin Willard.

1795   Kindey-dial shelf clock in mahogany case by Aaron Willard, Boston, Massachusetts.

1802   Pine-cased clock with one-day wood movement by Eli Terry, Plymouth, Connecticut.

1810   Eight-day lyre-style wall clock made by Samuel Abbot, Monticelier, Vermont.

1812   One day wood tall clock, with painted case grained to simulate expensive wood, made by Thomas & Hoadley, Plymouth, Connecticut.

1814   Tall clock with painted pine case and eight day wood movement by Joseph Ives, Bristol, Connecticut.

1815   Eli Terry's earliest shelf clock design in a simple box case.

1816   Gilt French figurine clock with likeness of George Washington, made for American markets by Jean Baptiste Blanc of Paris.

1819   Pillar and scroll clock by Eli Terry.

1820   Pillar and scroll clock, made by Seth Thomas, Plymouth, Connecticut.

1820   Joseph Ives mirror clock in gilt gesso made in Bristol, Connecticut.

1825   Unsigned gilt presentation style banjo clock made in Boston, Massachusetts area.

1826   Empire style shelf clock by Joseph Ives.

1830   Pillar and scroll shelf clock by Silas Hoadley.

1830   One-day wood-movement clock by E. Terry & Son, Plymouth, Connecticut.

1835   One-day wood-movement clock by Luman Watson, Cincinnati, Ohio.

1838   Mahogany veneered shelf clock by the Forestville Manufacturing Company, Bristol, Connecticut.

1839   One-day "hour glass" clock with wagon spring by Joseph Ives, Plainville, Connecticut.

1845   Fusee spring driven steeple clock with balance wheel escapement attributed to Silas B. Terry.

1845   42-inch tall empire clock with etched glass tablets by Forestville Mfg. Co., Bristol, Connecticut.

1845   One-day weight driven brass-movement clock by Chauncey Jerome, Bristol, Connecticut.

1847   One-day steeple clock with brass springs by Brewster and Ingrahams, Bristol, Connecticut.

1850   40 1/2 inch tall Empire-case clock with whistle pipe organ made by Kirk & Todd, Wolcott, Connecticut.

1851   Papier mâché shelf clock with mother of pearl inlay and painted decoration. Movement by Chauncey Jerome and case by the Litchfield Manufacturing Company.

1852   Eight-day shelf clock by Brewster & Ingrahams, Bristol, Connecticut.

1853   Thirty-day wagon-spring powered clock by Atkins, Whiting & Co., Bristol, Connecticut.

1854   Domed candle-stand clock with balance-wheel escapement by Terryville Mfg. Co. in Terryville, Connecticut.

1855   Astronomical regulator with mercury pendulum by Howard & Davis.

1860   Two-dial calendar clock made by Burwall & Carter, Bristol, Connecticut.

1860   "Venetian" style clock with Joseph Ives tin-plate, tin-wheel clock movement by N. L. Brewster, Bristol, Connecticut.

1865   A blinking eye clock with its case by Bradley & Hubbard.

1865   An iron front clock made by the American Clock Company.

1865   Theodore R. Tamby's patent globe clock manufactured by Lewis E. Whiting, Saratoga Springs, New York.

1865   An iron front clock, painted and gilded, made by the American Clock Company.

1865   Gilt column shelf clock with Ives rolling-pinion strap-plated movement made by S. C. Spring & Company, Bristol, Connecticut.

1866	Small OG case clock with spring-driven movement and label of Chauncey Jerome, Austin, Illinois.
1872	Wall hanging American regulator by E. Howard Watch & Clock Company.
1873	Watchman's regulator made by E. Howard Watch & Clock Co., Boston, Massachusetts.
1875	Eight-day calendar clock by Ithaca Calendar Clock Company.
1880	Walnut shelf clock by the William L. Gilbert Clock Company.
1880	"Ionic" gilt wall time piece with alarm made by E. Ingraham Co.
1880	Twenty-four inch dial "corrugated gilt gallery clock" by E. Ingraham Company, Bristol, Connecticut.
1885	Philosopher shelf clock by Ansonia Clock Co., Brooklyn, New York. Produced until after 1915.
1885	Regulator No. 4 made by William L. Gilbert Clock Company, Winsted, Connecticut.
1890	French style mantel clock with a bronze figure of St. George and the Dragon.
1890	Mantel clock in black marble case by The Waterbury Clock Company.
1890	"Bee" alarm clock with box by Ansonia Clock Company, Brooklyn, New York.
1901	"Defender" model oak wall clock by Waterbury Clock Co., Waterbury, Connecticut.
1901	"Monarch" model black-enameled case mantle clock with painted marbleized wood columns by E. Ingraham Company, Bristol, Connecticut.
1905	Dewey model oak kitchen clock made by E. Ingraham Company, Bristol, Connecticut.
1910	"Gloria" model swinging-ball clock by Ansonia Clock Co., Brooklyn, New York. Clock and pendulum both swing, pivoting on figurine's hand.

The National Association of Watch and Clock Collectors, Inc., or NAWCC, is the national organization for clock and watch collectors that sponsors educational meetings, shows, and seminars for it members. The association is located at 514 Poplar Street, Columbia, PA. 17512.

Clock Museums

American Watch & Clock Museum
100 Maple Street
Bristol, Connecticut

Henry Ford Museum
Greenfield Village
Dearborn, Michigan

Greensboro Clock Museum
300 Bellemeade St.
Greensboro, North Carolina

Museum of Clocks and Watches
New York University
Albany, New York

National Museum of Clocks and Watches
514 Poplar Street
Box 33
Columbia, Pennsylvania

Old Clock Museum
929 E. Preston
Pharr, Texas

Old Sturbridge Village
Sturbridge, Massachusetts

Time Museum
7801 East State Street
Rockford, Illinois

Henry Francis DuPont Winterthur Museum
Winterthur, Delaware

Clock Prices from the 1897 and 1927 Sears, Roebuck Catalogs

Alarm Clock

Beacon Luminous. Nickel Alarm Clock, with luminous dial; height, 6 1/2 inches; width, 4-1/4 inches; 4-inch dial, and is manufactured by the New Haven Clock Company of New Haven, Conn.; best grade lever movement. Price, 97c. Note: The dial on the clock is luminous, and will show distinctly the time in the dark. The darker it is the brighter it glows. Price Range: 78c to $2.62.

Porcelain Shelf Clock

Boudoir No. 10. Genuine Porcelain Case, ornamented with gilt and colored, hand painted decorations; height, 7 1/8 inches; length 5 3/8 inches; beveled glass, 2-inch silver dial; has fine lever movement made by the Waterbury Clock Company. Price, $2.50. Price Range: $2.15 to $8.25.

Iron Case Shelf Clock

Leona. Very fancy enameled Iron Case, showing variegated blue finish, in imitation of marble, with fancy colored and gilt ornamentations; height, 12 inches; width, 9 1/4 inches; 6-inch white or gilt dial; fine 8 day movement made by the New Haven Clock Company; strikes hours and half hours on cathedral gong bell. Price: $5.95. Price Range: $5.90 to $7.90.

Mantel Clock

Fresno. Very fine polished wood case, in imitation of black onyx, fancy gilt engraving, marbleized columns, with gilt bronze bases and caps, fancy sash; height, 10 3/8 inches; length, 16 inches; dial, 5 1/2 inches; fine eight-day movement; made by the Waterbury Clock Company, strikes hours and halves on cathedral gong bell. American white dial, Roman figures, or American gilt dial with Arabic figures. Price: $5.40. Price Range: $4.40 to $6.30.

Statue Clock

Knight. Elaborate gilt bronze case, with very fancy engravings and scroll decorations, ornamented with a fine statue of a bugler; very fancy sash, with fine visible escapement; height, 15 inches; width, 15 inches; has fine 8-day movement; made by the Ansonia Clock Company; strikes hours and halves on beautiful cathedral gong bell. Price: $14.85.

Oak Kitchen Clock

Clarence. Fancy Cabinet Clock, 22 1/2 inches high; dial, 6 inches; made in oak only; beautifully carved and ornamented; fine eight-day movement; made by the Ansonia Clock Company; strikes hours and halves on wire bell. Price: $2.75. Price Range: $2.00 - $3.90.

Walnut Parlor Clock

Buffalo. Fancy Cabinet Clock in solid black walnut only; very fancy ornamented and carved case; height, 26 7/8 inches; dial, 8 inches; fitted with fine eight-day movement; made by the Waterbury Clock Company; strikes hours and halves on wire bell with calendar. Price: $3.70. Price Range: $2.00 to $6.15.

Perpetual Calendar Shelf Clock

Fine solid walnut or oak case, elegantly carved, height, 24 inches, dial, 6 inches. This clock is made by the Waterbury Clock Company; has fine 8 day, hour and half-hour strike movements, with cathedral gong bell and calendar. The calendar is perpetual with a 6-inch dial, showing the day of the week, the month and day of the month; is guaranteed to be thoroughly reliable and accurate. Price: $5.25.

Weight Clock

This is the genuine old reliable Seth Thomas weight clock, made by the Seth Thomas Clock Company of Thomaston, Conn. The case has rosewood or walnut finish, with one day weight strike movement; height 25 1/2 inches. Price $5.20.

Octagon Lever Wall Clock

Has oak, walnut or cherry veneered octagon case or round nickel case; movement is patent lever, is made by the Waterbury Clock Company, and is a good reliable timepiece. This clock is especially desirable for offices, schools, churches, etc.; one day, with 4-inch dial, time only. Price: $1.45. Price Range: $1.45 to $4.90.

Ionic or Figure Eight Wall Clock

Saxon. Rosewood veneered case, well finished; height, 22 inches; dial, 10 inches; is made by the New Haven Clock Company, and is especially designed for offices, schools, churches, etc.; 8 day; time only. Price: $3.40.

Short Drop Octagon Wall Clock

Has solid oak or fine veneered case; movement is made by the Waterbury Clock Company and is thoroughly reliable. Is designed for offices, schools, or churches. 8 day, 10-inch dial; time only. Price: $3.45. Price Range $3.45 to $4.40.

Long Drop Octagon Wall Clock

Regulator. Has solid oak or handsome veneered and very fine finished case. Height, 32 inches, with 12-inch dial; has very fine 8 day movement, with calendar; made by the Waterbury Clock Company; has wood pendulum rod, which is not affected by changes in temperature, and is a very fine timepiece; makes a very fine office clock or regulator. Price: $5.85.

Wall Clock

Bruce. Oak, walnut, or cherry case, beautifully carved and turned ornaments. Height, 38 1/4 inches; width, 14 3/4 inches; dial, 8 inches; has fine eight-day movement with wood pendulum rod, which is not affected by changes in temperature; made by the Waterbury Clock Company, and is a very fine timepiece. Price: $6.70.

Cuckoo Wall Clock

These clocks are largely in use in Europe and have of late years become very popular in the United States. The clock is quite a novelty, but is thoroughly practical and is certainly a very interesting and pretty ornament in any home. The clock is fitted with a solid brass movement, cut steel pinions and has two copper finished fancy iron weights. The height of the case is 19 inches, width 13 inches, made of fancy carved German walnut, ebonized ornaments, has white bone hands and figures. Price: $5.50.
(The little door above the dial opens every half hour; a bird appears, flaps its wings and calls cuckoo, once for half hours and as many times as it is necessary to denote the time on the hours. Before the cuckoo has called the hours the clock strikes the hours in the regular way.)

Celluloid Shelf Clock

Boudoir Clock. Amber color celluloid, with green color front. Dial, 3 1/4 x 1 7/8 inches, length, 7 7/8 inches, height, 4 3/4 inches. 30-hour movement. Not an alarm clock. Price: $3.75. Price Range: $2.35 to $3.75.

Compressed Wood Shelf Clock

Here's the newest clock on the market. The case represents a beautiful bungalow in natural colors; even the foliage is colored to represent nature. It is practically indestructible; made of highly compressed wood pulp compound; carefully enameled in natural colors. The clock runs 30 hours with one winding. Does not alarm. Length, 9 3/4 inches; 5 1/2 inches high. Price: $2.95. Price Range: $2.95 to $3.45.

Tambour Shelf Clock

The Chevalier. Finished in rich mahogany, two-tone inlaid effect. 21 1/2 inches long and 9 5/8 inches high. Silvered dial is 6 inches in diameter with raised bronzed finish numerals. Louis XIV style hands. Price: $6.68. Price Range: $6.68 to $27.75.

Banjo or Williard Clock

This popular clock is as accurate as it is beautiful. Hand rubbed mahogany finish. 35 1/2 inches high and 10 1/8 inches wide at the widest part. Glass is decorated with decalcomania ornamentations. An attractive 6-inch silvered dial. Louis XIV style hands. An excellent eight-day pendulum movement insures accuracy. Strikes hours and half hours in sweet tone cathedral gong. Price: $13.90.

Glossary

Acorn clock: A clock whose shape resembles that of an acorn.

Adamantine: A patented colored celluloid applied as veneer.

Advertising clock: A clock used for promotional purposes on which the advertising may be found on the case, dial, or tablet.

Alarm: An attachment that rings or gongs at a selected time.

Animated clock: A clock that incorporates a lifelike movement characteristic of an animal or person.

Anniversary clock: A clock, wound annually, that runs for a full year. It is sometimes called a 400-day clock.

Apron: A decorative piece, sometimes used to hide construction details. It may be on the bottom of a case or between the legs of a floor or shelf clock.

Arabic numerals: Figures on a dial written 1, 2, 3, etc.

Arbor: The axle on which gears and pinions are mounted.

Arc: The swinging path of a clock pendulum.

Backboard: The inside back of a clock case where a label frequently was applied.

Balance: The oscillating wheel that, along with the hair-spring, regulates the speed of a clock.

Balloon clock: A bracket clock that is shaped like a hot air balloon.

Banding: A strip of veneer used for decoration on a clock's case.

Banjo clock: The name given to Simon Willard's wall clock, the "Improved Timepiece," because of its shape.

Barrel: The round container that holds the mainspring.

Beading: A type of carved or applied molding.

Beat: The ticking sound of a clock. When the ticking is consistently steady, it is "in beat." If it is irregular it is "out of beat."

Beehive clock: A clock with a rounded case that bears some resemblance to a beehive.

Bevel: A chamfer such as the angled edge on plate glass.

Bezal: A ring of wood or metal that surrounds and holds the glass over the clock dial.

Black clocks (or Blacks): Clocks made of marble, black iron, or black enameled wood, popular from about 1880 to 1920.

Black Forest clock: A clock made in Germany's Black Forest area.

Black walnut: A common wood used for clock cases.

Blinking eye: An iron statue clock with moving eyes. Also called a winker.

Bob: The weight at the bottom end of a pendulum rod.

Bracket: The part under the box on a Willard banjo clock.

Bracket clock: The British name for a shelf clock.

Brass works: A clock mechanism made of brass.

Bushing: The place where the arbor goes through the clock plate for its bearing.

Calendar clock: A clock that can indicate the day, month, and date, or combinations thereof, as well as the time. A perpetual calendar makes provisions for the various lengths of months and adjusts accordingly; a simple calendar must be changed manually to accommodate a change from a 30-day to a 31-day month as well as Leap Year changes.

Case: The housing for the works of a clock.

Celluloid: A trade name for the first artificial plastic, invented in 1869, that received wide commercial use. Some clock cases in the early 1900s were made of this highly flammable material.

Center seconds hand: The hand that is mounted on the center of the dial. Also called "sweep second hand".

Chamfer: A sloping or angled edge on wood or plate glass; a bevel.

Chime: The simple melody on the bells or gongs that sounds on the hour, or at the quarter and half hours.

China or porcelain clock: A clock with a case made of glazed porcelain.

Chronometer: An accurate time keeper.

Clock: A machine that records the passing of time and strikes at least on the hour.

Clockwise: The circular motion as the clock hands go around the dial.

Connecticut shelf: Any shelf clock made in Connecticut such as beehive, cottage, and steeple.

Cornice: The horizontal molded projection at the top of a clock case.

Count wheel: The locking plate that controls the number of strikes on a clock's bell or gong.

Crystal regulator: A shelf clock with glass panels on all four sides.

Date dial: An additional dial that shows the dates of the month.

Dead-beat escapement: A clock escapement that does not recoil (fall back).

Dial: A clock's face with numbers and hands.

Drum: In a weight driven clock, the round barrel on which the weight cord is wound.

Ebonized: A black finish that looks like ebony wood.

Eight-day clock: A clock that runs for eight days on one winding.

Escapement: The clock mechanism that controls the swing of the pendulum or the movement of the balance wheel.

Escutcheon: The trim around a keyhole.

Finial: A wooden or metal spire or turning.

Flying pendulum: Also referred to as Ignatz. A novelty clock invented in 1883 and made again in the late 1950s. Hanging from an arm, a small ball on a thread swings in a horizontal circle and is regulated by twisting and untwisting around vertical rods on each side of the clock.

Four-hundred-day clock: A clock, wound annually, that runs a full year. It is also called an anniversary clock.

Frame: The case of a clock.

Front wind: When a clock is wound through the dial.

Fusee or fuzee: A grooved cone upon which the cord from the spring container unwinds to equalize the force of the spring in a clock.

Gadget clock: A time keeper with extra accessories.

Gallery clock: An eight-day or electric clock, usually round, with a simple case and a dial usually eight inches or larger that hung on the wall in a public establishment.

Gilt: A gold-colored coating.

Gimbal: A support used to keep a clock level.

Gingerbread: The name used to describe the elaborate designs pressed into a clock's wooden case.

Gold leaf: An extremely thin sheet of solid gold sometimes applied as a decoration on columns, tablets, or other parts of a clock case.

Gothic case: A case, a variation of a steeple clock, with a pointed top that bears a resemblance to Gothic architecture.

Grandfather clock: The name for a floor-standing clock in a tall, upright case. Originally called a long-case or tall-case clock.

Grandmother clock: A smaller floor-standing version of a grandfather clock.

Hair-spring: A slender hair like coil that controls the regular movement of the balance wheel in a clock.

Hammer: The clock part that hits the bell or gong to indicate time.

Hands: The time indicators that mark the hours, minutes, or seconds on a clock dial.

Hanging shelf-clock: A wall clock with a shelf-like base that makes it appear as if it is sitting on a shelf.

Horology: The science of measuring time or making timepieces.

Hourglass: A device containing sand that flows from the upper to the lower globe to indicate an exact time.

Ignatz: See: Flying pendulum.

Iron-front: A shelf clock with a cast-iron front.

Kidney dial: A dial on a clock that resembles the shape of a kidney.

Kitchen clock: A clock frequently of oak, manufactured from the late 1800s to the early 1900s, that sat on a shelf in the kitchen.

Jack: A moving figure turned by a clock mechanism.

Leaves: The teeth of the pinion gears.

Lighthouse clock: The unique clock made by Simon Willard in 1822.

Long case clock: The original name for a grandfather clock.

Looking-glass clock: A clock with a box like case and mirror instead of a painted glass tablet.

Lyre clock: A form of banjo clock with a lyre shape.

Mainspring: The principal or driving power that keeps the mechanism running in a spring-driven clock.

Mantel clock: A shelf clock.

Marine or lever clocks: Clocks that operate with a hair-spring balance and continue to run when transported or set on an uneven surface (contrary to pendulum clocks). Often used aboard ships.

Marquetry: A decoration on wood achieved by inlaying wood veneers in various designs.

Mask: A human or animal face used as a decoration.

Massachusetts shelf clock: The style of clock frequently called half clock or box on box.

Mean time: When all hours and days are of equal time.

Medallion: An applied circular, oval, or square decorative turning used on a clock case.

Mercury pendulum: In American clocks, a silvery-looking, usually cylindrical pendulum that resembles French examples, which actually contained mercury.

Mirror clock: See Looking glass clock.

Mission style: A straight-lined, plain clock case that was popular from about 1900 to 1925.

Molding: A continuous decorative edging.

Moon dial: The dial at the top of a clock that shows the phases of the moon.

Movement: The "works" of a clock.

Musical alarm: An alarm that plays a tune on a small musical box. It was made popular from the late 1890s to the middle teens in the 20th century.

Novelty clock: A small, often animated clock, usually in the shape of a familiar object. OG, or ogee: A double, continuous S-like curve used as a molding on certain straight rectangular clocks of the early-1800s.

Open escapement: The wheel and pallet movement that can be seen on some clock dials.

Pallet: A catching device that regulates the speed of a clock by releasing one notch of a toothed wheel (ratchet wheel) at each swing of the pendulum or turn of the balance wheel.

Parlor clock: The older, carved-case, often walnut, Victorian clock of the mid-to-late 1800s that stood on a shelf or mantel in the parlor.

Pediment: An ornamental top on a clock case, frequently curved in shape.

Pendulum: A clock weight, often ornamental, hung from a fixed point so as to swing to and fro as it regulates the clock's movement.

Pillar and scroll clock: A shelf clock attributed to Eli Terry.

Pinion: A small toothed wheel driven by a gear.

Plate: The front and back of the clock's movement or works.

Position clock: Also called a regulator.

Regulator clock: Originally a term for any accurate clock.

Reverse painting: A picture or design often used on a clock tablet and painted on the back side of a glass in reverse order to a normal painting.

Roman numerals: Roman letters used as numerals on clock dials, as in I, II, III, IV, etc.
On older clocks, four was often represented by IIII, an old Roman numeral for IV. It is said that this form better balances the VIII on the other side of the dial.

Shelf clock: A clock designed to sit on a shelf or mantel.

Spandrels: The four corners, featuring painted designs or metal decorations, that square off a round clock dial.

Spring clock: A clock whose power is provided by springs.

Steeple clock: A clock with a sharply pointed Gothic case and finials at each side.

Sweep second hand: A hand that's positioned in the center of the clock and sweeps, in a circular motion, around the dial.

TP: An abbreviation for timepiece.

T & S: An abbreviation for time and strike.

Tablet: The front, lower glass, frequently painted, on a clock case.

Tall clock: A long-case, floor clock, often called a grandfather clock.

Tambour clock: A shelf clock, also called a humpback or camelback clock, with a case that is flat at each side and rounded in the middle.

Thirty-day clock: A clock that requires winding once a month.

Thirty-hour clock: A clock that runs for thirty hours without rewinding.

Time and strike: A clock that both tells the time and strikes or chimes.

Timepiece: A clock that tells time only and does not strike or chime.

Tower or turret clock: A church, steeple or public clock in a tower.

Train: The series of gears and pinions that carry the power to the escapement.

Verge: The pallet axis of a clock.

Visible escapement: Same as open escapement.

Wagon spring: A series of flat springs, attributed to Joseph Ives of Bristol, Connecticut, used instead of a coil spring to power the clock movement.

Wall clock: A clock that hangs on the wall.

Weights: The power source that drives the mechanism in a clock when it is not spring driven.

Winker: An iron statue clock with blinking eyes.

Zebrawood: An African wood, straw colored with fine stripes, that is sliced into veneers to cover an unattractive wood. Also called zebrano.

Bibliography

Books

Bailey, Chris H. *Two Hundred Years of American Clocks and Watches.* Englewood Cliffs: A Rutledge Book, Prentice-Hall: no date.

Brewer, Clifford. *Pocket Book of Clocks.* Country Life Books, an imprint of Newes Books, a division of the Hamlyn Publishing Group Ltd. Felthan, Middlesex, England: 1983.

Burton, Eric. *Clocks and Watches 1400-1900.* Frederick A. Praeger Publishers, New York and Washington, no date.

Distin, William H., and Robert Bishop. *The American Clock.* New York, NY: E. P. Dutton, 1976.

Drepperd, Carl W. *American Clocks and Clock Makers.* Garden City: Doubleday & Company. 1947.

Ehrhardt, Roy. *Official Price Guide to Antique Clocks.* Westminster: The House of Collectibles, 1985,

Ehrhardt, Roy, and Red Rabeneck. *Clock Identification and Price Guide.* Kansas City, MO: Heart of America Press, 1983.

Lloyd, Alan H. *The Collector's Dictionary of* Clocks. A. S. Barnes and Co., New York, NY: 1964.

Ly, Tran Duy. Clocks: *A Guide to Identification and Prices.* Arlington, VA: 1984.

Maust, Don, ed. *Early American Clocks.* E. G. Warman Publishing Co., Union Town, PA: 1971.

Mebane, John. *The Coming Collecting Boon.* New York, NY: A. S. Barnes and Company, 1968.

Miller, Andrew Hayes. and Dalia Marcia Miller. *Survey of American Clocks: Calendar Clocks,* Elgin, IL. Antiquitat, 1972.

Miller, Robert W. *Clock Guide Identification with Prices.* Des Moines, IA: Wallace-Homestead Book Company, 1974.

------------ *Clock Guide No. 2 Identification with Prices.* Des Moines, IA: Wallace-Homestead Book Company, 1975.

Moore, Hudson N. *The Old Clock Book.* Tudor Publishing Company, New York, NY: 1936.

Palmer, Brooks. *The Book of American Clocks.* New York, NY: The Macmillan Company, 1974.

-------------- *A Treasury of American Clocks.* New York, NY: The Macmillan Company, 1968.

Schwartz, Marvin D. *Collectors' Guide to Antique American Clocks.* Doubleday & Company, Inc., Garden City, NY: 1975.

Smith, Alan, ed. *The International Dictionary of Clocks.* London and Auckland: Melbourne, Singapore and Toronto: 1988.

Welch, Kenneth F. *The History of Clocks and Watches.* Drake Publishers, Inc., New York, NY: 1972.

Catalogs

Israel, Fred L., ed. *1897 Sears, Roebuck Catalogue,* New York, NY: Chelsea House Publishers, 1976.

"F. Kroeber Clock Co. Manufacturers, Catalogue of Clocks, " New York, NY: 18981899.

Ly, Tran Duy. *Chelsea Clock Co. Catalog E.* 1911. Arlington: Arlington Horology & Book Co., 1987.

Schroeder, Joseph J., Jr., ed. *1908 Sears, Roebuck Catalogue.* Chicago, Ill.: The Gun Digest Company, 1969.

Newsletters

"Eli Terry: Dreamer, Artisan and Clockmaker, "Bulletin of the National Association of Watch and Clock Collectors, Inc., summer 1965.

"The Welch, Spring and Company," Bulletin of the National Association of Watch and Clock Collectors, Inc., #12, February 1978.

Photo Index

Color Photo Index

Reference Guides for Collectors